The Canadian Small Business Handbook

Susan Kennedy-Loewen

Foreword by
John Bulloch
Founder of
The Canadian Federation of
Independent Business

KEY PORTER BOOKS

National Library of Canada Cataloguing in Publication Data

Kennedy-Loewen, Susan
    Guide to Canadian Small Business

Includes index.
ISBN 1-55263-402-7

    1. Small business—Management. I. Title.

HD62.5.K464 2001   658.02'2   C2001-901684-0

THE CANADA COUNCIL | LE CONSEIL DES ARTS
FOR THE ARTS | DU CANADA
SINCE 1957 | DEPUIS 1957

ONTARIO ARTS COUNCIL
CONSEIL DES ARTS DE L'ONTARIO

The publisher gratefully acknowledges the support of the Canada Council for the Arts and the Ontario Arts Council for its publishing program.

We acknowledge the financial support of the Government of Canada through the Book Publishing Industry Development Program (BPIDP) for our publishing activities.

Key Porter Books Limited
70 The Esplanade
Toronto, Ontario
Canada M5E 1R2

www.keyporter.com

Design and electronic formatting: Heidy Lawrance Associates

Printed and bound in Canada

02 03 04 05 06 6 5 4 3 2 1

To my mother, Marion Kennedy,
who taught me perseverance and passion for my work,

To David, my husband and best friend,
whose support and love have been my inspiration in life,

To my colleagues at Scotiabank,
whose everyday support has meant so very much to me,

And to Ron, Zhen and Wendy,
without whom this book would never have happened!

Contents

Foreword

by John Bulloch

**Founder and CEO Vubiz Ltd. and Founder and Past President of
The Canadian Federation of Independent Business**

If there is one common source of frustration for those who start and grow small companies it is dealing with people who do not understand what their world is all about. It can be an unsympathetic banker, an aggressive tax collector, a bureaucratic government regulator, a busy accountant, an expensive lawyer, politicians with their promises or just major corporations that want their business without understanding their needs. I often think of small business people as economic guerrillas trying to survive in a hostile environment.

Living in this environment creates a kind of small business subculture where trusted networks of advisers and suppliers help define the success of a small business. Really understanding small business is the secret of the Canadian Federation of Independent Business (CFIB), a small business advocacy organization I created in 1971, which today has 100,000 members. Every one of these members is visited personally once a year, and every action CFIB takes is directed by the majority vote of the members. CFIB has become a trusted part of the small business owner's network because CFIB listens to what they have to say.

Reading this manuscript to write the forward, I felt I was reliving my life working in the family business, Bulloch Tailors, an established Toronto custom-clothing business. It started with the passion and excitement my father had leaving a secure job with Eaton's department store in 1938. At the age of five, I remember running around the store while my father and his next-door neighbour were building shelves. Everyone was so excited. He told me later, when I could appreciate these kinds of things, that he'd decided to operate a cash business and focus on customer value. He made one sale the first week he opened, and when the customer demanded credit, my father turned him down. It was a gutsy decision, but as he put it, "You only go out of business when you run out of cash." At the age of ten, I was on the cash register meeting the customers and doing endless chores. These are my most precious memories. A small business is never easy to describe or study because of all the informal family relationships it comprises. Mother worked on the books. All my father's brothers were brought to Canada from Belfast and started their life here working in the family business. As my three younger brothers grew up, they did their own apprenticeship in the factory and on the sales floor. We developed very close relationships with the employees, who became an extension of the family.

What I found of special interest is the time my father spent building relationships with all his advisers and suppliers. This started before he opened his own shop, something that was five years in the planning stage. The founder of Tip Top Tailors, for example, gave my father a large oak table as a gift when he opened the store. It was there for more than 50 years. Every week I worked there, my father took me to meet the bank manager. And here there was a trusted relationship and friendship that lasted for more than two decades.

What a difference from the situation today, when small business banking officers too often move up the ladder as soon as they start to understand their local clients. Father had taken courses in basic bookkeeping at night school before opening his business. As he so cogently put it, "It is important to know what you don't know."

After, we visited our major suppliers—companies that manufactured his suits, wholesalers of British woollens, suppliers of linings and threads and so on. What an adventure! His philosophy was always to treat suppliers well because they were the best source of market intelligence and technical advice. By selling for cash he was able to pay his suppliers on time and enjoy discounts for fast payment.

My father built his business selling officers' uniforms during World War II, and I travelled to the camps on the weekends, where he would take orders and his customers' measurements. Selling uniforms was not something he planned for in 1938, but an opportunity he jumped on when Canada entered the war. The opportunistic nature of small business is another one of its defining characteristics.

He wouldn't be making much profit selling uniforms, but he believed that if his customers survived he would have them as clients for life. His instincts were solid, because the business customer base for the next 40 years comprised all those who'd worn his five-piece uniform, which they had bought for only $200. These garments are part of our history and are still in the attics of veterans and their children across Canada.

Over my father's lifetime, he never stopped selling and serving customers. Everything starts with marketing and sales, he said. "You can't be an expert in every area. That is where you have to rely on a good bank manager, a good accountant and good suppliers."

Susan Kennedy-Lowen makes her contribution—educating small business owners and all those who want to service the small business community. She obviously walks the small business walk and talks the small business talk. She would be a trusted banker and advisor for any small business owner.

1 A Canadian Dream:
Owning Your Own Business

Small business is the backbone of the Canadian economy, creating more than 300,000 new jobs every year for Canadians. Many Canadians dream of owning their own business, and in fact, one in six working Canadians owns his or her own business. And why not? Canadians are hard-working, honest, straightforward people, willing to take on a challenge, solve a problem, and seize an opportunity—all great qualities for business owners.

If we could distill the Canadian business market down to precisely 100 businesses with the existing ratios remaining the same, the list would look something like this:

- 77 small businesses would be making annual revenues of less than $1 million
- 44 small businesses would be making annual revenues of less than $250,000
- 97 businesses would have fewer than 50 employees
- 69 small business owners would depend on their business as their sole or most important source of income
- 50 small businesses would have been started from scratch
- 20 small businesses would have been bought from someone else
- 6 businesses would be family inheritances
- 53 businesses would have no employees outside the owner
- 25 small businesses would be in their first year of business; 20 of the 25 businesses would successfully make it through the first year
- 37 businesses would be expanding
- 52 businesses would be owned or co-owned by a woman
- 6 businesses would be selling on-line
- 20 businesses would be owned by Canadian immigrants

In the past ten years, small business in Canada has grown by more than 40%—there are more than 2.1 million businesses in Canada, and more than 2.3 million Canadians describe themselves as self-employed; one in every four households in Canada has a small business owner in it. They are on every street and in every town and city all across this country.

The great range of business interests and business volumes represented by those 2.3 million Canadians cannot be overlooked, and when I use the term "small business," those are the people I'm referring to. We might also define a small business as one that has revenues of $1 million or less a year—77% of the business population falls into that category. We can also define a small business in other ways: as a business that employs five or fewer employees or a business whose results are achieved primarily by the owner. So you can see, no matter which way you approach it, these self-employed business owners are a force to be reckoned with!

> Don't let fear and "common sense" hold you back. Go for it.
> —Colin Fraser, Porcher Investments Ltd.

Why is owning a business so attractive to so many people?

- Some people see an opportunity and act on it. Many corporate and wage-earning employees wait for the right opportunity and the right timing to start their own business. Retirement, layoffs, accepting a package to retire early, all can create the right time to leave. I know many people who start their planning early, so they are ready to move when the opportunity presents itself.
- Some are looking for a better way to use their skills—they know they can deliver a product or service faster, cheaper, and more effectively than is currently being done.
- Some want to take control of their lives, what they do, when they do it, how they do it, and why. Going out on their own gives them better control over their financial future.
- Downsizing has led a number of people to start their own businesses as a way to use their unique skills and knowledge. It doesn't happen as often as you might think—only about 15% of small businesses are started as the result of downsizing. Most people who own a business are doing it because they want to.
- Flexible work schedules allow for a better balance of life. No matter what the age or gender, many people need more time at home with their families. Stay-at-home parents caring for young children or for an elderly parent find self-employment fits well with their

other responsibilities. Some people are looking for a sense of fulfillment and achievement. Running a part-time or full-time home-based business can be the answer.

- Many people like self-employment for the independence it gives them.

The individuality and uniqueness of every small business makes them interesting and exciting. The fact that you *can* make your own decisions, and that your business *depends* on you making a decision, gives you a sense of control and independence you aren't likely to get working for someone else.

I grew up surrounded by small business. My parents farmed in central Alberta, as did many of my family members. My brothers and sister have all owned or own businesses—my aunts, uncles, cousins, friends, neighbours were or still are business owners. My elementary school playmates were the sons and daughters of the butcher, the baker, the jeweller—all small business owners in my small town.

This book is about what I have learned from small business owners that I have had the privilege and joy of knowing, not only in my personal life, but throughout my twenty-plus years as a banker at Scotiabank. It is about the fundamentals of how to be a successful business owner *on your terms*, as you strive to build a successful business and maintain a happy and balanced life.

> **It is a myth that many small businesses go bankrupt each year. In 2001, fewer than 1 in every 200 businesses went bankrupt. Many business owners close their business operations every year, not because the business failed but because they found a better opportunity or the business had successfully served its purpose.**

Four Cornerstones to Success

Small business owners consistently point out the same cornerstones as the key factors in their success:

1. The business owner
2. The team
3. The customers
4. The suppliers

I'll talk about each of these in greater detail throughout the book, but they're worth introducing here. The first is about you, the business owner, and the effect owning a small business can have on you and your family.

Your Life

Many people who own businesses, whether large or small, cite a desire for independence as one of the reasons for setting out on their own. They're looking for freedom from the restrictions of others' decisions, freedom to set their own hours and working conditions, and to decide priorities. But one self-employed person I know says wryly that owning your own business gives you the freedom to work seven days a week. And it's true—many small business owners find they are putting in longer hours than they did as paid employees. The big difference is that they love it!

Some small business owners aren't even aware that they're working 60 or 70 hours a week, which often becomes a problem. You may get so caught up in running your business that friends and family begin to take second place—a far distant second place. It doesn't happen on purpose, of course, but the effect is the same. Your life becomes unbalanced—all work and no play. You may not think of it as work—you're out there making calls, talking to suppliers, writing reports, or performing another of the many responsibilities you've taken on as you wear all the hats in your company. It's exciting because you start to see the payoff for this dedication. But your friends and family will notice your absence. If you have even the slightest inclination to be a workaholic—and many small business owners do— you'll take it to new heights as the owner of your own business.

Making your business a success is important, no doubt about it. But so is the other part of your life. Learn to schedule time off. Because you *are* your own boss, you can decide when this time will be. It doesn't always have to be on a weekend, though if your spouse has a regular nine-to-five job or your children are in school, weekends may be the best time to make a date with your family. If your spouse is either self-employed or works on weekends, catch a Tuesday afternoon matinee together every week, or go out to dinner with friends.

If you live alone, it's even easier to work all the time. It becomes a point of pride to show your friends how hard you work, so you stop going to the weekly trivia contests at the corner bar, or you give up your yoga class because you don't have time to relax any more. Everything feels just fine to you, because it's normal to eat, drink, and breathe your business. But there's another normal out there—it's the big world where friends socialize, families eat dinner together, and people take holidays and pursue hobbies.

Share your plans and goals with those who can help you reach them, and you might find getting there easier. Get the commitment of your family, your mentors, and members of your team to support you in your endeavours. That includes encouraging them to remind you when it's time for you to take a rest. What could be better than a satisfying business and personal life over which you have optimal control?

Your Team

As a business owner, you are taking two paths at the same time—you have set your sights on achieving your personal dreams and goals—owning a house, retiring at 60, sending your children to university—and achieving goals for your business. The sooner you establish your team to help you reach these goals, the greater peace of mind you can have. Chapter 5 focuses on your relationships with people such as your banker, your lawyer, your accountant, and your marketing expert. The number of people will vary, depending on the type of business you do; you may also have a financial planner, and of course there are your mentors and the network of associates you build up over time. No matter how small or large your team is, each member should be a good listener who will work with you smoothly, quickly, and effectively. A good sense of humour never hurts either.

> **Networking is an important activity for small business owners. Because you sometimes work in isolation, be sure to set up a network of people in the same line of business. How? Attend meetings, conventions, seminars. Hand out your business card to everyone you meet. Tell people what you do.**

One of those team members will be your banker. Depending on your own skills, you can get along without a bookkeeper and accountant, and some businesses don't need lawyers. But everyone needs to deal with a bank, although we don't all need a banker. I'm differentiating here between a bank, the place you deposit and withdraw your money, and a banker, the individual in the bank with whom you will do business for your business—open an account, negotiate a line of credit or operating line, secure a credit card for your company, help you with your investments, and most important, get to know you and your business. Your banker should be more than just a money person. This professional should want to know about *you*, and what you want to achieve. Look for someone who shows a real interest in your business and be prepared to explain the finer details of your enterprise. Convey your excitement and passion to the banker, share your business plan and ideas, and discuss what you hope your business will achieve for you.

The relationship you are undertaking is a professional one, but it is also very personal and private in nature. The information you share with your banker will help her to help you understand your business goals. Your banker is the expert in banking, but when it comes to your business, *you* are the expert—whether it's market gardening, pottery making, or graphic design. Together, you and your banker will be asking, "How do we do what's right for my small business?"

Early in my banking career, I learned that it is extremely important for all bankers to understand what their small business client is looking for in the relationship, and work to deliver it. Years ago, I met Clem Gerwing and his son Tim, owners of Alberta Boot in Calgary, a company that manufactures great Western boots and ships them all over the world. One of our first conversations remains a guiding principle for me to this day.

Clem was quick to point out to me, "It is only three steps farther for me to walk to the Royal Bank than it is to the Scotiabank, and I am up to it." What did this mean to me? It meant I had to earn the respect and business of every customer who was dealing with me, and I had to keep working to keep that business. What did it mean to Clem? It meant he understood the value of his business and the importance of his relationship with the bank.

Both Clem and Tim have had various "bank experiences," which they shared with me. They remembered bankers who gave them good advice, and those who gave them questionable advice. ("Well, it's easy to increase your bottom line, just sell more boots" was the unhelpful advice from a banker who didn't last long.) Most of all, people like Clem and Tim know the bankers who went to the wall for their business—the advocate, the ally, the banker who refused to accept the wrong answers.

I learned how important it is for all bankers to understand what their small business client is looking for in the relationship, and work to deliver it. Like Clem and Tim, you shouldn't expect any less from *your* banker.

Your Customers

Owning a small business is an evolutionary process. As opportunities arise in the marketplace, you adapt and change to seek out the best ones. Whether you are in your first year or your tenth, focus on your customer, because big or small business, we are nothing without a customer.

When potential small business owners investigate whether their idea will stand up in the marketplace, they usually call it market research. It's more productive to think of it as "getting to know your customer" and then "getting to know your customer all over again." The more you understand your customer, the more efficiently and effectively you can deliver. Knowing your customers and their needs confirms that your new products or services will hold up in the marketplace, or that you still have a customer base for the products and services you offer today. It helps you focus on selling what your customers want, not what you *think* they want.

Even if you instinctively know who your customers are (this is likely to be the case when you're starting a business because you see an opportunity or need), checking out your instinct is a worthwhile exercise.

Let's look at a couple of different types of customers. You've just invented the next Trivial Pursuit, and you know who your target market is—people in the age range of 20 to 50—with a certain disposable income and a certain education level. This is the "target market," the end-user of your product, and therefore your customer. How are you going to reach your customer? By selling your product to the Bay, or other retail outlets that handle games— they too are your customers. In this example, you have two customers with two very specific sets of needs and values—one is the end customer, the other is the retailer who also sells to the end customer. You need to make sure you understand them both.

Once you know who your customers are today and who your *potential* customers are, you need to have a plan to reach them. Do they want you to go to them, do they want to order by phone, do you need the current storefront location you have, should it be bigger, smaller? These are all questions you need to ask when you're starting up, and throughout the life of your business.

Whether you are a new or existing business, take a fresh look at your customers and reassess how you deliver your products or services; this way, you can determine if your approach to them is still the best way, or if you need to make some changes.

Your Suppliers

After your customers, your suppliers are key to the success of your small business. After all, the business of a business is selling something (a product or service) to someone (your customer or client). You need to identify who your suppliers will be and determine how confident you are about their ability to support your business's success.

If you are a new business ... Who will your suppliers be for that great new game you've invented? Who makes those little game pieces? Who makes the boards? The fancy boxes they all go into? Who designs them? If you manufacture a unique gauge used in the oil industry, where do you get the raw products to make the gauges? Do you already have contacts with your suppliers because you're familiar with the industry? Have you chosen the best one?

The key is to establish strong relationships with your suppliers, making sure they are financially sound and capable of meeting the needs of your business and reliable in their delivery, billing, pricing, and service.

People who are in the knowledge-based or information-based business don't have to worry about suppliers to the same extent as those in more traditional businesses, like manufacturing. They are selling information, research, services, or skills that don't rely on the manufacturing process. Their major suppliers are likely to be their Internet service provider (ISP), the local Business Depot or Staples, and other knowledge workers. Their business is very different than a manufacturing or importing business, but it's a small business nonetheless, and faces the same need for reliable, dependable suppliers.

If your business is experienced ... Ask yourself, are the suppliers you use today the best suppliers for your business for the long term? Are you doing the right thing for your business? Are new options available that you should consider?

Maintaining your relationships with your suppliers has been critical to your success so far. They have likely helped you through some tough times, whether it was providing a fast, big order for a new customer, or offering support during a period when your business slowed down. I'm not suggesting you give up what works, only that you reflect on whether your business has changed and whether your suppliers provide what you need for what your business does *today*.

Depending on the field you're in, you might want to research new supplier opportunities, both in your community and abroad. The Internet has been a great tool for business owners, who can now access information on new suppliers quickly, easily, and at a time that is convenient for them.

2 Start-ups

You're starting a business from scratch because you have a dream, and you've been able to bring together your idea and your skill with an opportunity. To many bankers, a "start-up" is a company that has been in operation less than two years. But the definition can go well beyond that. I have often heard people use the term to define a business that has been growing ever since its inception, even though it has been in business for more than five years!

Five Start-up Tips for Small Businesses

1. Drive, dedication, and commitment—intangible and unquantifiable— are important qualities to make your business succeed.
2. Know your business by doing your research well. No business fails because the owner knows too much.
3. Know your market.
4. Create a business plan (see Chapter 4).
5. Meet your banker. Even if you don't need to borrow money now, your relationship with your banker can be invaluable.

Buying a Business or Franchise

Most small business owners in the start-up phase already know what their business will be—the product or service they'll be selling. If you're less certain of the business you want to develop, or unsure of the commitment you want to make in getting a new business off the ground, you could look at buying a business or buying into a franchise system; a franchise is a business in which the products or services sold are controlled by the franchisor (Wendy's and Tim Hortons are examples of franchises). The business ideas are already established: contracts with suppliers, inventory control, and profit margins. Both routes have advantages and disadvantages, as follows:

- Buying an existing business can cut down on some of the risk associated with starting a new business as you're more likely to see a return on your investment fairly quickly as revenue streams have been established. However, you may also be paying for the intangible of goodwill—the business's reputation and customer base—an expense a new business does not carry.
- You have an opportunity to review the history of the business you're thinking of buying to assess its stage in the life cycle of any business—start-up, growth, and maturity. You should also, with the help of your lawyer, make sure there are no liens against the company and review any existing contracts that will be in effect when you buy the business.
- You can decide to buy only the assets of the company or, if it's an incorporated company, the shares (as well as the liabilities).
- You may be able to get financing more easily because of the track record of the business or franchise system.
- Franchises are for individuals who like to operate in a highly structured environment in which expectations are clearly set out and ongoing support is usually available. However, there is not a lot of room for entrepreneurship in a franchise. For many potential small business owners, this is a large drawback, for they are looking to spread their wings and try out their own ideas. But franchises offer people who desire structure the opportunity to operate a business themselves, with support and guidance from the franchisor, who often has years of experience. Be warned, though, that you should investigate the franchisor thoroughly to be sure you fully understand what you are committing to.
- Buying a franchise can be a complex process. Some franchisors will not allow any changes to the contract, so be sure to work with a lawyer who has experience in this area of the law—don't use the lawyer who did your will for you (you do have a will, don't you?) or drew up your mortgage papers. You need to know exactly what the rights and responsibilities of each party—both franchisor and franchisee—are.

- If you are seriously thinking about a franchise, visit other franchise owners of the same chain and get their opinion on whether or not it's a good investment—they are usually very candid.
- If you want to buy an existing business or start a franchise, you'll need to do some preliminary investigation into the business or the franchise system you're interested in (see Chapter 11 for information to help you assess any business you're buying). This means putting together a team, similar to the team you'll need for any new small business—at least a lawyer and an accountant (see Chapter 5). If you have the financial resources to buy a business or franchise, you should spend the few thousand dollars it might cost to consult with your lawyer and accountant, both of whom should be experts in the field, especially if you're buying a franchise. This is money well spent even if you walk away from the opportunity; in fact, that few thousand dollars could save you hundreds of thousands if you find something not to your liking.
- Spend a week at the premises and see the operation. Verify that volumes are truly as stated. Talk with customers, ask what they like and don't like, gauge their loyalty.

Of all the businesses in Canada, 69% were started from scratch—they weren't bought from someone else and weren't franchises.

Starting a Business from Scratch

There are many important issues to consider as your business is starting up. One of them—the team of experts you'll be putting together to advise you on particular issues—is so important I've devoted a whole chapter to the topic. (Chapter 5: Relationships.)

For now, let's concentrate on other practical matters. Before you make a final decision on them, however, talk them over with your advisers to make sure you haven't overlooked any factors that might have a negative impact on your new business.

Size
Many small business owners are seeking the freedom and independence owning their own business can give them. Thinking about hiring people

to help out is the last thing on their mind. And this isn't a bad way to start—starting a business can be stressful enough without the responsibility of being sure you can afford to pay another person. But to be sure you're right, ask yourself a few questions. Why might you need employees? How many could you manage and afford to pay? Will you need full-time, part-time, or contract help?

You may not know the answers to these questions until you've been in business for a while, but review them on a regular basis. Perhaps you'll find there's some part of your business that is always a chore for you to do. Is it bookkeeping? Is it sales? Is it collecting your accounts receivable from your customers? Can your business sustain the expense of paying someone else to do these tasks, either full-time or part-time? If you're in a growth phase and are contemplating hiring new employees, how much new business can these new employees generate? For example, say you have a landscaping business; you can't keep up with demand for your services, but you don't want to restrict your ability to add to your client base. You begin to think taking on some help would be a smart move. Ask yourself: Can I increase the number of clients sufficiently to cover the costs of my new employee or will the new employee just help me keep my head above water with my existing clients?

> **Eighty percent of all small businesses have fewer than five employees. More than a million businesses have at least one employee.**

Hiring an employee will allow you to improve your lifestyle, give you the chance to take a holiday, or spend more time with your family. You will need to do a cost comparison to determine the drawbacks and advantages. Let's look again at the landscaping business example. If the landscaper adds the cost of the employee—say, $30,000 per year—the cost of the loppers ($125), and the rake ($75), can he make more than $30,200 in new sales? If not, he has diminishing returns. However, the landscaper can now spend his freed-up time finding better ways to make money (collecting receivables, finding new customers, growing more business from existing customers). But don't forget, you're talking more than money on this one. The decision to hire an employee may be a "quality of life" issue. You might have decided the only way to achieve a balanced life is to hire someone to help you in your business. You can't put a dollar value on your leisure time but you can do some number crunching to see how to free up time by hiring someone to help out.

When do you know it's time to hire a new employee? Well, if your significant other doesn't recognize you any more, it may be a sign. Your business plan can also help you work through this question (see Chapter 4). Review your goals as you reassess what you want to achieve by owning your own business—independence, control, a better work-home balance. As you

> Reality is not 8:00 a.m. to 5:00 p.m.
> —Perry Hulowski, Perry's Automotive, Prince Albert, Saskatchewan

think about whether you should be growing, ask yourself when you want to retire; calculate where the business cycle is. All these issues must be addressed when you review your size and your decision to grow. Becoming an employer is a big step and will change the dynamics of the way you operate (see Chapters 7 and 8 for information on hiring staff and growing your business).

Premises

In deciding where to base your business, ask yourself the following:

- Where will your business be?
- Will you operate from your house or work from an office?
- Will you rent or buy premises from which to operate your business?
- How important is image to you and your business? What image do you have to portray?
- Are your customers coming to you or are you going to them?
- Who are your customers and what do they expect?
- What is the cost of an office? It can be high compared to the return you get for it.

Let's look at three options: operating out of your home, leasing or renting premises, and buying premises.

Operating out of your home   Many small businesses operate from the owner's home. It could be for reasons of economy, but also for more personal reasons—to be home with your children, to be able to look after an elderly parent, or just to be able to spend more time in your own home. You might need to do a bit of renovation to turn a corner of your basement into an office, but if you're someone such as a researcher, architect, musician, or consultant, your office needs may be minimal—a phone with voice mail, a fax machine, a computer, a filing cabinet, and a desk—and some musical instruments for the musician, of course! Some small business owners attend meetings only at the clients' premises or, in fact, never meet the client, doing all their business with the aid of phones, e-mail, and couriers (for example, translators). In addition, commuting time becomes a non-issue, and it's easier to keep your hours flexible when your office is just down the hall or up a flight of stairs. Moreover, the Canada Customs and Revenue Agency (formerly Revenue Canada) allows you to expense a portion of your household expenses as business expenses—mortgage interest payments, property tax, and heating are three of the most common ones.

Some municipalities have bylaws prohibiting home-based offices, so make sure you check. Be considerate of your neighbours. If your business is going to generate a fair amount of foot or vehicular traffic, your home may not be the best place for your business. Operating your business from your home doesn't mean you should be any less businesslike in your approach. You still need to think through a business plan (Chapter 4); you still need a team (Chapter 5); and you still may need to borrow money (Chapter 3).

Renting your premises   In some businesses, it's important to have public exposure—for example, a hairdresser or real estate agent who may rely on walk-by traffic to acquire clients—so renting or buying space is a given. A lease could be one of your biggest expenses, so shop carefully for your space as it also commits you to that property for an agreed-upon period of time. Before signing any lease agreement, ask your lawyer to review it. A little good advice goes a long way. Renting business premises differs from renting residential premises. You are likely responsible for renovating the premises to your needs.

Buying your premises   Although buying their premises seems like a good idea to many small business owners, in fact, it can be one of the riskiest of all choices. Business failure is frequently caused by high rent or mortgage payments. When you buy, you have to put some of your own money into the purchase, which depletes your capital, leaving you less to operate with. Your money is permanently tied up in bricks and mortar, and this can really put a damper on your ability to grow, be flexible, and take advantage of opportunities that suddenly arise. On the other hand, your cost is fixed and therefore more controllable—there's no landlord to suddenly raise your rent or change the conditions when the lease is up. You might even become a landlord, but be absolutely sure that you like the idea of being a landlord—owning property and renting it out can become another small business.

If you're contemplating buying your premises, think ahead to what the future might hold. Ask yourself: What will happen when it comes time to sell the property? Will your property have retained its value? While it's true that land is one thing they're not making more of, in the cold hard world of real estate, prices don't always rise. The area you've bought in may not always be the desirable location it is today. Twenty years from now, it might be a backwater of commerce. The community that seems vibrant and poised for growth today may be hit badly by a downturn in the economy or changing land use in your neighbourhood.

It's especially important, when you are starting your business, to keep your costs under control and minimize your long-term commitments to expenses such as buying property. Consider such expenditures only when you are really comfortable that all the excess cash you have sitting around cannot be used better in other ways, such as nurturing the parts of your business that bring you revenue and profits. You also need to consider whether you plan to have your business as long as you will have a mortgage on the property!

The average life of a business is six years.

Structuring Your Business

How you will structure your business is not something you spend much time thinking about in these early exciting days, but once you're ready for your first "deal," it takes on some importance. Most small business owners choose a sole proprietorship as their business structure because is it easy and inexpensive; it takes minimal time and cost to set up. It's important to know what the other options are—the partnership and incorporated company—and the advantages and disadvantages of all of them. If you need someone to bounce ideas off, talk to other small business owners, your banker, and your lawyer. If minimizing taxes is important to you, you should definitely talk to your accountant, who can guide you on the tax differences of each type of ownership and its implications for your particular business. If your goal, like most owners, is to minimize the amount of tax you pay, your accountant can be your best friend. A colleague of mine, whose husband owns his own graphic design business, says that no matter how good they are at completing their financial statements and tax returns, their accountant always finds at least one more way to save them money!

Unincorporated—Sole Proprietor

As a sole proprietor, you are simply an individual carrying on a business activity in your own right. You make all the decisions associated with the business and are completely entitled to the benefits deriving from the business. You collect all the rewards for owning the business, whether they be financial or personal rewards. You also bear full responsibility (liability) for all the costs, losses, and obligations that your business undertakes. There is no distinction between the personal assets of the sole proprietor and those of the business. You personally own what the business owns, and you personally owe what the business owes.

You look first to your own resources to finance your business. If friends or family provide capital (that's cash!) to your business, they do it in the form of a loan, just as the bank would. They will expect, at some point, that you will pay them back.

You still have to satisfy all the federal, provincial, and municipal requirements to carry on your business—things such as registering your business name, buying a business licence from the municipality or province. In addition, you need to be aware of and meet any specific regulations that involve your industry (for example, handling of dangerous goods). If you hire staff, you must live by employment legislation (see Chapter 7 for information on becoming an employer).

Advantages of a sole proprietorship

- The cost of getting your business structure off the ground is kept low—you don't need to invest a great deal of your upfront cash into getting started. It's simple and easy to get your business under way and to maintain it once it's up and running.
- You won't have to be concerned with as many regulations as apply to other business structures. Your record keeping can be kept to a minimum—the only reason you need it is for you, the tax department (CCRA), and anyone you borrow money from.
- All the profits go to you.
- There can be tax advantages to being a sole proprietor because you can claim any business losses against other income you may have, which can reduce the taxes you pay.
- You are in complete control of your business. You get to make all the decisions!

Disadvantages of a sole proprietorship
- As a sole proprietor, your liability is unlimited—your entire personal fortune stands behind your business.
- As the sole proprietor, you bear full responsibility for the debts you take on for the business
- If you go on holiday or fall ill, there's no one to keep the business running (unless you have an employee).
- Some government programs aren't available to sole proprietors.
- Self-employed people aren't eligible to collect Employment Insurance (EI) if their business fails, unless they have also been working elsewhere as an employee while running the business.
- You have to make all the decisions!

Registering your sole proprietorship   You may operate the business under your own name or a name you've chosen, but if you use a name other than your own, you should register it with your provincial registration agency (there's a small fee). Whichever you choose, the business's income and your income are considered the same and are taxed as personal income. The business expenses you incur are deductible against this income. You can open a bank account for your business, either in your own name or under the name of the business without being incorporated. In fact, it's always advisable to keep your business and personal expenses separate. It makes for easier bookkeeping. Pay yourself from your business, putting the money into your personal account to use for your personal expenditures—food, housing, clothing, and savings.

> To get information about registration regulations in your province, go to www.cbsc.org/osbw/busforms.html and click on your province. If you live in Ontario, you can register your business on-line. Go to www.cbs.gov.on.ca/obc/. In Nova Scotia, register on-line at www.gov.ns.ca/snsmr/nsbr/.

Partnerships

From early times, people have found it advantageous and more efficient to pool their talents and resources by forming a partnership. Partnerships are essentially groups of people acting together for a business purpose with a goal of making a profit. It is important to know that the partnership formed is not a legal entity separate from the people who make it up.

The Partnership Act varies little from province to province. Whenever two or more people carry on business in common with the desire of making a profit, a partnership exists. It doesn't mean that profit was made, only that it was the objective. It means

- there has been a joint contribution of capital (cash) to establish a business;
- there was an intention to share expenses, profits, or losses, and
- there was joint participation in the management of the business.

Partnership agreements   A partnership relationship is primarily one of contract, usually created by an agreement, either verbal or written. While a partnership agreement will not have an effect on the relationship between the partners and outsiders, it can significantly change the rights and obligations of the partners between themselves.

It is important for the partners to have an agreement that sets out the exact nature of the relationship between them. With a written document, there is less likelihood of disputes. For example, each partner, individually, can make decisions on behalf of the partnership, from signing a new contract to borrowing money to hiring staff. Your agreement can spell out when and how each partner should be involved in these types of decisions. Your partnership agreement can also specify that one partner will bear all or a significant portion of any loss because that person is better able to do so.

Unless you are extensively familiar with the Partnership Act, have a lawyer review the final agreement you and your partner have drawn up.

The partnership agreement should

- set out the duties of each partner in the business activities (for example, either person can sign cheques for the partnership, but both must sign to borrow money)
- define the type of work or talent each partner is expected to contribute
- specify the amount of time each partner is willing to commit to the business (at least a minimum amount!)
- show how profits are to be shared
- show how capital is to be distributed

- describe any limiting powers or authority of each partner
- include methods to resolve disputes
- set out the terms under which the partnership would be dissolved

The liability of each partner is not restricted to just the contractual obligations of each partner but also the noncontractual obligations and actions taken on behalf of the company. In other words, all partners are liable for the wrongful conduct of the other partners as if they had committed the act themselves. This also applies to liabilities incurred by the business—that is, by *any one* of your partners acting for the business—in all business-related activities, whether you were responsible for making the initial decision or not.

The sole proprietor's liability is unlimited—your entire personal fortune stands behind your business. You are responsible only for your own conduct and decisions. In a partnership, the partners' liability is unlimited and each of you is responsible for the others' conduct. Therefore, if the business assets of the partnership are not sufficient to satisfy any claims of those you owe money to, the partners must pay out of their own personal assets in the same proportion as they share profits.

In a partnership, the business is similar to a sole proprietorship in that it does not operate as a separate entity and therefore does not pay tax as a separate entity; each owner reports profits and claims expenses according to the percentage of ownership.

Partnerships and sole proprietorships compared   Most of the advantages and disadvantages of the sole proprietorship apply to a partnership, with these differences—first the positive:

- You have an extra source of capital.
- There are more hands to get the work done.
- There is a broader knowledge base for management—each partner may bring different skills and experience.
- Establishing a partnership can be less expensive than incorporating.
- Record keeping can be minimized to satisfy only the partners, and a few government agencies (like the tax department) and those you borrow money from.
- Many tax advantages available to corporations are also available to partnerships.

And now the cautions:

- Because there are two or more people, there will be two or more opinions on virtually every issue. If you're not good at negotiating, conflicts will arise.
- It can be hard to find a partner who matches your enthusiasm, drive, and interest. Many partnerships dissolve because one person felt she was doing 90% of the work and receiving 50% of the reward.
- And to repeat a point I made already, one partner can bind the other without the other's approval. You need to have a partner you really trust or you could be leaving yourself vulnerable.

Limited Partnerships   A limited partnership is an extension of a general partnership. It comprises general partners, as above, who manage the company, and limited partners, who contribute money (capital). The limited partners are liable only for the amount of capital they have contributed, while the general partners are liable for all other debts and obligations. The general partners, who have unlimited liability, usually receive more of the profits. The limited partners cannot be involved in managing the business.

To qualify as a limited partner, the partnership must abide by the governing legislation. If limited partners fail in any way to follow the provisions set out, the usual outcome is that they are deemed to be general partners with all the consequences accompanying that designation. That means that while they had attempted to limit their liability, their actions of participating in management or decisions have deemed them a general partner. They then revert to all the liability and responsibility of a general partner.

> The term "silent partner" usually refers to a limited partner— someone who contributes money but cannot be involved in decision-making.

The sole advantage of a limited partnership is that it allows the partner designated as "limited" to invest money in a partnership while avoiding the general unlimited liability that goes with being a general partner. Again, if the idea of a limited partnership is of interest to you, your lawyer can help you set out or review the agreement.

Incorporation

The concept of the incorporated company was created to respond to large companies that needed a way to obtain great amounts of capital through the participation of many people. Large companies needed to have lots of people participate in the business financially without playing active roles. The incorporated company achieved this goal.

The most significant feature of the incorporated company is that it becomes a legal entity unto itself, separate from the people who own shares in it. The shares represent each individual's interest in the corporation and can be bought or sold, so shareholders can buy and sell shares without affecting the ongoing operations or decision-making process of the business. This structure is therefore more flexible in meeting the business requirements and more effective when more capital needs to be raised.

Because your business is now an entity of its own, it has a unique set of rights and responsibilities. The business is liable for everything it owns and is responsible for everything it does. Incorporation brings with it more rigorous reporting requirements.

The owners of the business are the shareholders. If you are the only owner, you will be the only shareholder. As a shareholder, you have no personal liability for the company's debts; liabilities are limited to the assets of the company (unless you provide your personal guarantee). You can retain profits to reinvest in the business or distribute them to the shareholders as dividends (the money a corporation pays to its shareholders).

You can incorporate through a lawyer who will set up a numbered company or you can do the registering and incorporating yourself. Lots of "do-it-yourselfers" pick up a kit at the local bookstore and do the incorporation themselves. If your business structure is going to be fairly straightforward (one or two shareholders), this route can be a good one. If you plan on accelerated growth or have a more complex business structure from day one, you might want to get your lawyer involved straightaway.

This is a good time to choose the lawyer who will be working with you and your business. Your lawyer or accountant can help you choose the appropriate structure to minimize both your business and personal taxes. Most lawyers will do the whole package: getting your GST number (see below, under "Other Start-up Issues"), registering your business, registering your business name.

Registering your incorporated company Registering your business as an incorporated company includes defining such things as the following:

- The name of the company
- The authorized share capital (total value of the shares that can be sold)
- In some provinces, the objects of the incorporation (why it was created)
- How shares are to be issued and transferred
- When meetings of the board of directors and shareholders will be held, and voting procedures
- Regulations covering borrowings, powers of the directors, and other officers
- How dividends will be dealt with, regulations concerning company records, and how shareholders will be contacted
- Who the initial shareholders are

Your company will receive a certificate of incorporation by filing the articles of incorporation and paying a fee. Only when you have legally incorporated can you add the words "Limited," "Corporation," or "Incorporated" or their abbreviations (Ltd., Corp., Inc.) after your business's name. These additions (called a suffix) should appear on all legal documents and on your company letterhead.

Advantages of incorporation

- Because the corporation is its own legal entity, its existence will continue past the involvement of any of the shareholders. If retaining control of your business is important to you, be sure you are the only shareholder or that you maintain at least 51% of the shares.
- The shareholders have a limited liability—limited to the amount they invested. They are not personally liable for the debts and other obligations of the corporation. If the total assets of the corporation are not sufficient to satisfy the obligations, the creditor demanding payment cannot turn to the shareholder for the difference, unless that shareholder has provided a personal guarantee to the debt.
- You have more options on how to withdraw money from your business. Your accountant can help you determine if you should take wages, a bonus, repayment of your shareholder loans, or dividends—all have different personal tax implications.

- There could be other tax advantages. At the very least, the share-holder can leave profits in the company and use the shares as an investment vehicle, deferring personal taxation to a later date. However, it is really important that you seek the counsel of your lawyer, accountant, and personal financial planner to ensure you have the most appropriate and effective long-term tax planning in place for your circumstances.
- Because your incorporated business is a separate legal entity, it does not suffer from the normal frailties of humans—it cannot "die." A corporation does not cease to exist unless you take specific steps to end its existence. If a partner dies, the partner-ship ends; when a sole proprietor dies, so does the business usually. The death of a shareholder (even if that individual is the sole income-generating source of the business or owns 100% of the shares) does not affect the existence of the business entity, only the operations. If the 100% owner of the business is not actively engaged in the business, the business can carry on indef-initely without the shareholder. The shares are simply treated like any other asset the deceased shareholder owns.
- The ownership of the business can be separated from the managing of the business. In a sole proprietorship, the business is controlled by the proprietor; in a partnership, each partner has a role in the business decisions. In an incorporated company, it is possible to separate owning the business from running the business. Share-holders do not have to devote time or attention to managing but can vote to change management should they not be happy with the results. And if you have 100% ownership, your vote counts in a big way!

Disadvantages of incorporation
- There are clear government regulations an incorporated business must adhere to. Ensuring you are compliant with these regula-tions can be time-consuming, and much more record keeping is necessary.
- Of the three types of structure, it's the most expensive to put into place and to operate.
- Dividends are taxed twice, once in the hands of the corporation (dividends are paid out of the after-tax profits of the company) and once in the hands of the shareholders (even if you are the only shareholder.) This is because you are now personally enjoying the

profits of your business. Generally, dividends enjoy a lower tax rate and can be a good personal financial planning tool.

- There are times where the incorporated structure does not limit your personal liability. Most financial institutions will request your personal guarantee for loans for your business. You commit to the bank that you will personally repay the debt if the business can't.
- Directors of the business can be held liable for activities of the business.

The decision to incorporate is not one to be taken lightly if you are the owner of a small business. However, the trend to incorporation continues to rise, primarily because of the tax advantages, the effect of global commerce, and the attraction of limited liability. Nevertheless, because many small businesses thrive on the flexibility afforded by sole proprietorships or partnerships, just under 50% of all businesses choose these structures.

Some individuals—such as doctors, dentists, lawyers, and accountants—cannot incorporate or derive no advantage from doing so. If you fall into one of these professional categories, check with your lawyer about regulations in your province.

Other Notes on Starting Your Business

The following are topics relevant to all business owners, no matter how long they've been in business. Sometimes you'll want to review chapters to remind yourself how you made decisions, reflect on your thinking as you got your business going, how committed and determined you were. The business of running a small business depends on looking to the future and revisiting the past now and then.

If you expect to have revenues of more than $30,000 a year, you'll need to collect the GST. If your revenues will be less than $30,000, you can still choose to collect the GST; some small business owners decide to do this because it makes them appear more credible and it has the added benefit of allowing them to be reimbursed the GST they pay on goods and services they buy to run their own business. You need to register with Canadian Customs and Revenue Agency (**www.ccra-adrc.gc.ca**) to get your business number, which will be part of your GST number. CCRA will send you the forms you need to fill out to remit your payments quarterly. *The GST you collect is not your money*, and it's advisable to keep it in a separate bank account so you can remit what is owed to the government after you've calculated what you can claim back.

If you will be accepting payments from your customers by credit card, you will need to establish an account with each merchant—Visa, MasterCard, and American Express—that you intend to accept payments from.

When you make a sale that is paid for by credit or debit card, the money from the sale can be deposited straight into your account with the bank. Some institutions will deduct their fees upfront while others collect them at the end of each month—taking the payment right from your account. Note that by having the fees deducted at the end of the month, you have use of the money for the month, and your daily reconciliation will be easier. You will get a statement on your merchant account activity outlining the transactions each month. Fees and equipment rentals are usually deducted from your account as well.

The bank will charge you fees for

- setting up the merchant accounts
- transactions—a percentage of every sale (sales made over the Internet, mail orders, and telephone orders may carry a higher fee because the customer has not signed the transaction slip)
- equipment rental; if your merchant account is used only for on-line sales, be sure you're not charged for this as you don't need the swipe terminal
- chargebacks, which occur when a transaction has been disputed by the customer

You may also have to deposit money that can be used as a security deposit once you've been approved; an Internet-based business may have to deposit a larger amount. Work with a knowledgeable banker in order to establish the best plan for your business and minimize your costs.

3 Where Do I Get Money?

No matter how small your business, you're going to need to spend some money to get started and to continue running your enterprise. You'll need office supplies and possibly furniture; you'll need to do some marketing; you may need to invest in equipment appropriate to your needs—a potter's wheel and a kiln, or a forklift, trolleys, and padded blankets for a moving company. As time goes on, you may want to expand, or perhaps you find yourself stretched now and then as you wait for customers to pay. Getting money to finance your business can be key to its success, so let's look at the variety of options available to you, from the traditional loan, to finding ways of managing your business, to freeing up more cash.

You, the Owner

Whether you are starting up a business or have been in business for many years, the primary source of cash for your undertaking is *you*. When you start, you are going to have to put some of your own assets to work—cash, equipment, your home, your investments. As your business grows and prospers, you will often need to decide if you should invest additional capital (cash or resources) to help your business thrive. Above all, be prepared to make some long-term and short-term investments into your business.

Loans

Most people who own or are about to own a small business will be familiar with the process of borrowing money—anyone who's bought a car will have likely financed the purchase through a bank, trust company, credit union, or a finance company like GMAC. These are also the companies you should consider when borrowing money for your business.

Operating Lines

You may want to set up a line of credit, also called an operating line, on which you can draw money as you need it. Lines of credit are normally used for day-to-day expenses (payroll, rent, inventory) to cover short-term needs while you are waiting for money to come in from your customers. You apply for it in the same way you apply for a loan. Lines of credit are established with a set limit, and you pay interest charges monthly. Expect to pay a small monthly maintenance fee.

Lines of credit operate in combination with your business account, so that when you make a deposit, it pays down any outstanding credit line, and when you overdraw your account, it advances money from the credit line. The advantage of a line of credit is that you make payments only when you use it, and the payments are in relation to the amount owing (the more you owe, the more interest you pay each month). The interest rate usually fluctuates because it is tied to the prime lending rate. How your rate will be set will depend on how you secure the operating line.

Establish your line of credit early in your business so that it will be ready when you need it most. It's also good to establish your credit rating as early as possible. It takes a little time to get an operating line in place; by the time you gather the information you need (most recent tax return, for example), make your application, and finalize the paperwork, the best part of a week may have gone by. Most banks can get a decision to you in a couple of days, but to save the sleepless nights, get it in place early. Knowing your line of credit is there when you need it is just good planning. Then, when you need to call on it, you'll already have done the right thing for your business.

Term Loans

Term loans are often used to purchase equipment. Their advantage is that you can match the repayment of the loan to the income the equipment generates. For example, if you buy a new industrial lathe for $30,000 to make wooden furniture, that lathe will help your business make furniture for three or four years. The lathe will start to make your business money as soon as it starts making furniture, but it likely will not pay for itself in the first few months. You want to make sure that you are matching the timing of the payments to the time the equipment is earning you money and that the payment schedule matches the life expectancy of the equipment—by the time the equipment is worn out, you want the loan paid off. Payments are usually made monthly on term loans. Term loans are also used for making leasehold improvements (such as renovating your rented or owned business premises), injecting capital into your business, or buying real estate.

The word "collateral" might come up in your discussions. If you have collateral to secure your loan, the banker will probably offer you a lower interest rate than on an unsecured loan; after all, the risk the bank is taking is offset by the risk you're taking in using property or other goods to secure your loan. Unsecured loans may be offered if you're a known customer with a history of loyalty to your bank, if your financial picture is sound, and if you have a good history of repaying your debts.

Another source of money for business owners who are starting up, expanding, or undertaking business improvements is a program called the Canada Small Business Financing Act (CSBFA). Under the CSBFA program, the federal government partially offsets any potential losses that the lender may take. This means that owners don't have to provide personal assets as security to support their business-financing efforts, though your banker might ask for a guarantee for a portion of the loan. The program is available to small Canadian businesses with less than $5 million in annual revenues. CSBFA loans can be used to finance

- the purchase or improvement of real property or immovables (such as large equipment)
- the purchase of leasehold improvements or improvements to leased property, and
- the purchase or improvement of new or used equipment.

Any of the purchases financed this way must be used for the business.

The maximum loan allowed is $250,000, and the loan can finance up to 90% of the cost of the asset. For each loan, the lender pays a fee to the government based on the amount of the loan. This cost is normally passed on to the business borrowing the money and can be added right onto the loan. The fee is usually around 2% of the loan amount. Interest rates charged are usually a little higher than you would normally pay for a bank loan, but they are very reasonable. The government has a cap on the rate to ensure the interest charged is not excessive. Apply for this type of loan through any bank.

The most traditional way of financing your business is through the bank—after all, you already will have a bank account—that's how you pay your personal bills, deposit cheques, get a letter of credit, and get approved for a credit card. I'm going to talk in more detail about your relationship with your bank later in this chapter, but first let's look at a few more ways of coming up with money for your business.

> **If you're self-employed and applying for a loan or line of credit, take your most recent income tax returns to show your small business banker what your income has been over the previous few years.**

Second Mortgage

Your house or other property can act as a source of cash for your business. Some small business owners will take out a second mortgage on their house, cottage, or other property. This is one of the cheapest ways to borrow money for your business. The bank is more likely to give you their best interest rates for small business lending when a residential property is used as security. It's a good trade-off for many business owners, especially when you're thinking about the bottom line of your company. Every dollar you spend in interest is a dollar out of your profit. That brings home the effect of interest payments in a pretty profound way, doesn't it?

How much you can borrow will depend on the equity—the difference between the value of your property and what you owe on it—you have in the property you're using as collateral. But you've built equity in your home—take advantage of what it can do for you. Not only will the interest rate be more attractive, you can spread your repayment over a much longer period. This can benefit how you manage your cash flow for your business—you can minimize the amount you're paying out in loan payments every month and maximize the opportunity to grow and sustain your business. Don't forget though—if you fall behind in your payments, you risk losing the property.

Talk to your banker about other options based on the same idea. Scotiabank offers a program called Scotia Total Equity Plan (STEP), which allows you to set a global borrowing limit, based on the value of your property. As a small business owner, you can use STEP to borrow for personal needs or for your business at the most attractive rates available—again, because property is used as security. As you pay down your balance, the global limit stays in place and you can borrow back up to the original amount when you need to.

Leasing

Another way of "getting" money is to avoid tying up your cash in large dollar purchases. By leasing—equipment, cars, office or factory space—you're not spending large amounts of cash on these items and leaving yourself short to cover supplies, payroll, marketing, not to mention your personal expenses such as your mortgage. Let's look at some of the other advantages of leasing:

- There is no prepayment of taxes; you pay the GST and PST (provincial sales tax) as part of the monthly rentals. When you buy, you pay these taxes upfront—a big chunk of money that could be going to run your business.
- Your operating line is preserved. Cash and lines of credit are valuable for the day-to-day needs of your business; don't tie it up with fixed asset purchases or in a down payment for a loan to buy a piece of equipment.
- You can enjoy tax benefits. You can deduct the lease payments as operating expenses.
- Pay as you profit and help protect the profits of your business by matching the timing of your revenues to the timing of your expenses. Leases are frequently spread over a longer period than a loan, so monthly payments are likely to be lower. Like a term loan, you can match the timing of your payments to the timing of your revenue—only your payment will likely be lower on a lease.
- Leasing is also a great way to get capital into your business. You can even take a piece of equipment that your business is now using and lease it back to your business (called a sale and lease back). This can give you an immediate injection of cash, which you repay over monthly payments. Leasing companies are very

familiar with this process and will be more than happy to talk to you about this option.

In a typical leasing example, you buy a $20,000 piece of equipment that you expect to last four years. You expect it to make you $10,000 in revenues each year.

Cost of equipment	$20,000	
Revenue generated	$40,000	in four years
Net benefit to you	$20,000	

You lease the equipment for 48 months at $535.20

$535.20 × 12 payments = $6,420.00 annually expensed

	Year 1	Year 2	Year 3	Year 4
Revenues	$10,000	$10,000	$10,000	$10,000
Expenses (lease)	$ 6,420	$ 6,420	$ 6,420	$ 6,420
Gross Income	$ 3,580	$ 3,580	$ 3,580	$ 3,580

If you buy the equipment for cash, you have to lay out $20,000 upfront. Your revenues each year stay the same, but you do not have the ability to reduce your income by the $6,420. You would have a gross income of $10,000 on which your business pays taxes.

Your accountant can advise you whether leasing or buying gives you the best value.

Credit Cards

More than 70% of all small business owners use a credit card to finance some or all of their business financing needs. They use it as a short-term temporary source of cash, in place of their line of credit, to make small equipment purchases and to cover immediate expenses.

Using a credit card for purchases on behalf of your company gives you instant credibility—someone else has already approved your credit card application and set you a credit limit. When you pay for purchases with a credit card, the suppliers you deal with can be assured they will receive their payment. Using a credit card is an easy and simple way to get established, and most cards give you a grace period of 18 to 26 days before they start charging interest. However, the usual warnings regarding credit cards apply: pay off as much as you can each month, ideally the entire amount; and don't be tempted to run your bill up to the limit just because you can.

Because banks recognize the importance of small business, some now offer business credit cards. You can borrow at rates equal to your line of credit—prime to prime plus 4.5% at the time of writing—and still enjoy the 26-day interest-free grace period. You receive the added value of having your name and your business name imprinted on the card. One of its greatest features is that if you are too busy, you don't have to move the balance to your operating line to save money, since the rate is equivalent in many cases. Check with your bank to see if they offer a similar card.

> Keep all your credit card bills for income tax time to remind yourself of your expenses and purchases made. You may also be able to claim the proportion of interest charges that correspond to the business-related expenditures on your bills.

Pensions

Some people use a lump-sum pension payment from a former employer to finance their start-up business. Many of my friends have either left their corporate job to start their own business or are just waiting for the "golden handshake" to make it happen. The planning can take years as they wait for the right time to make the move. Many new business owners have prior corporate lives and are now successfully launched into their own business. It is a myth that they took up business ownership because they were "laid off," "couldn't find a real job," or "they'd run out of options." Very few business owners have chosen to be self-employed as a last resort.

It's possible, but not always advisable, to withdraw money from your existing Registered Retirement Savings Plan (RRSP). For salaried Canadians, RRSPs are a long-term retirement savings plan. For many small business owners, RRSPs are a way to minimize taxes by deferring taxation to a time when they most need the cash. I know many small business owners who have withdrawn money socked away in RRSPs to inject cash into their business, paid the tax on the withdrawal, and moved on. For them, the RRSP was a savings vehicle for the day their business would need it. But do be careful. The RRSP withdrawal cannot just be "replaced." Each year, you are allowed to contribute a percentage of your income to your RRSP, and once you have done it, that's it. If you take money out, you can replace it only if you have not already used your contribution limit for that year. So if your RRSP is really part of your long-term retirement plan, as it is for many of us, make this decision with your eyes open.

When you withdraw money from your RRSP, a certain amount will be withheld for taxes at release of the funds; you will need to include this withdrawal as income in your income tax return for that year; and, of course, the money is no longer working inside your RRSP to provide you with retirement income. However, angels (see below) can use money from within their own self-directed RRSPs to invest in your company because it is regarded as a true investment rather than a loan or withdrawal. A program exists that allows self-directed RRSP holders to use funds inside their RRSPs to purchase shares in an incorporated small business. The owner of the RRSP cannot have any interest or participation in the activities of the business. Speak with your accountant for more information or Canada Customs and Revenue Agency. Your accountant or your lawyer may also be able to connect you with wealthy investors seeking new opportunities for their money.

> **A self-directed RRSP is one you manage yourself. You make all your own investment decisions, researching and monitoring your investments.**

Finally, you can withdraw money from your RRSP in the form of a loan—to finance your education or buy your first home (Home Buyer's Plan), for example. By choosing the right use for the funds, you may have found a more appropriate way to get the money out, and get it back in, without the tax implications.

Angels

An angel investor—either an individual or group of individuals—is someone who provides capital investments to early-stage or growing companies. This is often referred to as "patient" capital, since it allows businesses a bit of a "payment vacation," that is, some time to grow before the money needs to be paid back. Accountants often know of angels looking for ways to minimize their tax by investing in small companies.

Because you're dealing with an individual, who is less structured and bureaucratic than most other lending institutions, there may be more room for flexibility in the terms. However, an angel investor is likely to want a contract that lays out the investment, the terms of repayment, the date by which the loan has to be paid off, and other relevant and specific details. Remember, though, that by borrowing from an angel, you're not likely going to have to relinquish control of your business. As with all contracts, however, make sure you clearly understand the terms and conditions, when you have to pay back, and at what cost.

Family and Friends

Your family is probably full of angels—people who want to help you financially with your business but who don't want to be involved in running it. Beyond your family, you may have a circle of friends, or friends of friends, or even total strangers, who are looking for ways to invest in a small way to encourage and support small business.

When you borrow from family or friends, make sure all the details are well spelled out in your agreement. The best way to keep your family a family is to write down the details of your arrangement. Let there be no room for misunderstanding or assumptions. You're more likely to go to family or friends when you're on financially rough seas, so the risk of misconceptions and conflict is higher. You don't want to end up losing both your business and your friends or the goodwill of your family member. Be prepared to help them understand your business, why you need the money, how you plan to use it. If you have a written business plan (see Chapter 4), show it to them just as you would show any other lender.

Partners

If you decide that you don't want to go to a bank or use any of the above methods of raising cash for your business, you might consider taking on a partner. Or you might find that after you've been in business for a year or two, you would like a partner for financial as well as other reasons. Not only will your new partner bring along cash, this person will also bring an extra set of hands, eyes, fresh ideas, and new networks to your business. (See Chapter 2 for more information about partnerships.)

Getting Cash from Your Business

No matter how long you've been in business—a day or ten years—there are times when you feel you're always running short of the cash you need to run your enterprise effectively. This is when business plans go out the window and reality sets in.

The first place to look for the cash you need is from inside your business operations. It might not come in the lump-sum form of most traditional loans, but by altering a few of your business practices, you can help your cash flow and free up some money. Most of the practices outlined below are ones you may think you are already following, but sometimes we lose sight of these fundamental principles, so it's not a bad idea to review them now and then, to ensure you're getting all you can out of your business.

Accounts Receivable

First, look to your accounts receivable (the amount owed by your customers for goods or services), a place where quick cash may hide. The longer it takes your customers to pay you, the less cash you have to pay your bills. Think of it this way: if your customers are taking more than 30 days to pay, you have just become a bank to them!

When you make credit arrangements with your customers, you establish how and when they pay you. By making sure you collect your money on time, or by renegotiating this period, from say, 90 days to 60 days, or 60 days to 30 days, you can increase the amount of cash you have on hand. Remember, accounts receivable means you expect to be "receiving" the money. If your customers aren't good at paying on time, you might need to move them onto a cash-only basis, only accept payments by credit card, or not offer them credit at all.

The goal is to arrange for money to come in from your customers before money has to be paid out. This way you won't be in the position of having to borrow to tide yourself over while waiting for your customers to pay you. When business owners get busy, paperwork is the first thing to fall behind, and if you don't know who owes you, or how long they have owed you, you may be losing out on the best way to get money for your business. Collect what is owed so you can pay what is due!

Look first at the customers who are overdue with their payments and follow up to see what the problem is. For some small business owners, this is one of the hardest things to do—a visit with a banker somehow seems preferable to giving customers a gentle reminder there's money owing. If time is an issue, consider paying someone to do this task for you. For customers who are still within the agreed terms, offering discounts can be a worthwhile tactic to tempt them to pay earlier.

How can you get your account receivables collected?

- Do it yourself. No one is more connected to the money owing to you than you.
- Hire someone part-time to collect your receivables for you.
- Pay your bookkeeper to do it.
- Pay your accountant or CMA (certified management accountant) to do it.
- Factoring is another method that provides short-term financing. Instead of pledging your receivables to the bank for a loan, sell the accounts receivable (at a discount) to a "factoring" company. You pay the factoring company a fee, but you do not have to concern yourself with collecting your accounts, or face the risk of a bad debt. Your customer's payments go to the factoring company instead of to you. There is definitely a cost associated with this approach, but if you can still make money by paying the cost, you may want to consider this option.

Accounts Payable

Next, look at your accounts payable—the amount your business owes to a supplier for goods and services. Can you negotiate longer credit terms? For example, you now pay your supplier within 15 days of receiving the invoice, but they allow you to pay at 30 or 60 days without an interest penalty. Are you taking advantage of this opportunity? Can you negotiate for even longer terms, without paying any interest penalty to the supplier? Also, check invoices to see if your suppliers offer a discount for early payment; if you have the cash available, pay in time to take advantage of the discount.

It's amazing what 15 days on either end can do for your cash management. If you can gain 15 days in the time you are paid, and extend 15 days on the time you pay, you will increase your cash in your account and even reduce the amount of interest you pay to the bank because you are not drawing as much (or at all!) on your operating line.

Deposits

If you're in a business such as home renovations, you're going to have to spend money on supplies before you're able to bill the customer. To avoid spending money from previous jobs on the supplies for a new job, explain to the customer at the time you're doing the estimate that you expect a deposit if you get the job, and make it clear that the deposit will go to purchase the supplies you need to get the job started. After all, if you don't have that deposit in hand, you are the one who will have to finance the supplies for a job that may be months away from completion and final payment.

Progress Payments

See if you can tie interim payments to dates of completion of work or delivery of service. In the home renovation business mentioned above, you could tie interim payments to the completion of new wiring and plumbing being installed, then drywalling and installation of new windows being completed.

Inventory

Check out your inventory. Understand how much inventory you need to complete just-in-time delivery, then see if you're overstocked. Controlling your inventory is efficient but it can also be difficult to do. However, carrying an extra 10 to 15% in inventory can rob your business of much-needed cash and can be costly, so it's worth the time to take charge. If you have too much inventory, get rid of it—find out if you can return it, sell it to another company that does similar work to yours, or offer it at bargain prices, then stay on top of it. If inventory control starts to stretch you too thinly—if you're on the road drumming up new business or staying up until midnight already preparing this season's catalogue—it could be time to take on staff to do the task for you. (See Chapter 7 for information about hiring staff.)

And of course, watch your buying habits. I liken inventory control to my grocery-shopping habits. If I don't take stock before I go, I end up with another box of crackers sitting on my shelf next to the other three. This kind of shopping uses money that I could use some other way.

Your Prices

Over the life of your business, things change—utility prices go up, your rent goes up, the cost of your inventory or providing your service increases. Have you passed on those costs to your customers, or are they eating away at your profits and your cash? It may be time to raise prices or rates. If you lose a hard-to-manage and high-maintenance customer due to price, could you replace them with two or more new customers that give you better value?

Work through the price/value equation. Over time, you are gaining experience and expertise, and the value of your knowledge increases. Have you adjusted your prices appropriately? Do you understand what the market will bear? This concept of maximizing your pricing is of special importance to service providers, who may find it hard to decide what their services are worth. It may feel dangerous to charge more than "the going rate" in your field, but if your clients value your work, they are likely to accept an increase in your rates. It never hurts to do a price comparison with your competitors to see where you fit in the marketplace. Don't just assess the value of your product or service, but the value you personally bring to the equation.

Venture Capital

Another category of lender is the venture capitalist, or investor. These are individuals or companies that have excess retained earnings and are looking for a good investment (sounds great, doesn't it?); they could be holding companies (a company formed to hold the shares of other companies, which it then controls) looking to diversify; they could be companies formed for the purpose of investing, or providing venture capital, for tax reasons; they could be people who are seeking ways to reduce their high taxes. A venture capitalist will usually "take" an equity position (shares) in your company.

Venture capital provides tailor-made equity for growing companies. Because many venture capitalists take an equity position in your business, you give up full ownership and some control of your business. When companies go looking for venture capital, they're usually ready to expand or buy out another company. Although there are many venture capital companies in Canada, your challenge will be finding one to assist with small business. Business Development Bank of Canada (BDC) is a good example of a company that provides financing for the small and medium business market. They consider not only asset-based decisions (using your accounts receivable, inventory, and fixed assets) but also the quality of management, historical performance of the company, cash flow, and broader industry trends when they make their decisions.

Your Banker

No matter where you get the money you need, your banker is going to be an important person in your life. Often, your banker can ask questions you haven't thought of, suggest areas and opportunities for you and your business, and generally be a sounding board for you.

Making Your Banker a Partner

Sadly, many people see their relationship with their banker as an adversarial one, with an expectation that the banker is going to try everything possible to avoid lending them money. It's true that in the past, banks have not always acted respectfully, thoughtfully, or with due consideration. I'm happy to say that times have changed, especially where small businesses are concerned. Banks have recognized that small businesses are big business for them and have gone to great lengths to understand how to better serve this market. So when you're shopping around for a banker, approach this experience as though you are looking for another ally to help your business's success.

> Consider your banker as a business partner. Your banker can help with many aspects of your business, and the more your banker knows about you and your business, the more value you will receive.
> —Alan Carson, Carson Dunlop, Toronto, Ontario

If you already have an established relationship with a bank, start there. Up to now you may have dealt with tellers, the automated teller machine (ATM), or the personal banking officer who helped you when you bought your home, but it's time to get to know others in the bank. And it's time for your contact in the bank to get to know you and your business. Some banks have dedicated positions to serve the needs of small business owners. These people act as a gateway for both personal and business needs. Be prepared to tell your banker about your goals for your business—and not just the financial goals. Share with her the passion you have for your business, how you want to treat your customers, how you want to treat your employees. Describe some of your customers; outline what you've done so far to accomplish your goals. Help her understand how your business goals tie to your personal goals, financial and otherwise. Invite her out to your premises. Keep her informed of little milestones—a new customer with a big order, and even more important, the second order from that same customer!

If none of this works to establish a good relationship with your banker, shop around for another one. Find a banker who has the same kind of passion for small business banking that you have for your business. If your banker doesn't want to listen to you talk about the business, you should be talking to another banker. Your business is bound to experience ups and downs, and when your banker understands what might be affecting those ups and downs, she is more likely to provide options and ideas to help you succeed. And you're less likely to receive an impersonal call requesting that you pay off your line of credit.

Keep your banker current about your situation. When you surprise him with bad news, expect a very important question: "What's been happening?" So make it a practice to meet with your banker regularly (monthly or yearly, depending on you and your business needs) to update him on what your business is doing. You don't need to be borrowing money to have these meetings.

When your business is growing and you need to do a new business plan, involve your banker in the process. You may be pleasantly surprised to learn there are new ways to save your business money, and new products or services that can save you and your customers time or make you more money. Your banker also provides a great networking opportunity. You may be surprised to find out that your banker knows someone or another business who can use your services.

A Successful Relationship

You're embarking on a relationship with your bank. You want it to be a mutually trusting relationship. This means that the banker needs to know about you, as well as your business. The more the banker understands about you as a person and as a small business owner, the more she will be able to help you and offer advice.

What are the kinds of things the banker will want to know about you?

How you define success. Success is defined differently by different people. Perhaps you want to eke out of your business enough money to live in the house *you* want to live in, provide for your family the way *you* want to, take vacations the way *you* want to, retire when and how *you* want to, be in business to do the things *you* want to—reaching these goals will mean you've been successful. So make sure the banker understands what you want and works to help you achieve it, even if her definition of success is different than yours.

Your business plan and the plan for your business. How will you make money? Are there are peaks and valleys in the type of business you're undertaking? What is the prospect for growth? The banker needs to know how your venture is going to help you repay the debt you're taking on—when you buy that piece of equipment, how does it generate income? You can help the banker understand how your plan will help you accomplish your goals (this is a useful exercise whether you're going to a banker for money or not).

Be prepared to answer some hard questions. The banker may play the devil's advocate—not to be suspicious but to understand the whole picture. The goal should be to save you time and money, help you seek methods that are a better fit for your business and direct you to others who can help you find solutions to your particular challenges.

Providing options and solutions. If you are declined for a loan, you have a right to know why. There isn't a banker I know who enjoys saying no to a customer. And there isn't a customer I know who enjoys hearing it. You may feel offended and personally rejected, but you need to find out why. Focus on the task at hand: finding out why your request for a loan was turned down. It's important to remember that it is not *you* who has been declined, it is the specific request for money that has been turned down. Any banker worth her salt will be ready and prepared to help you understand why. Then deal with the issues, not the emotions.

Many times, requests for money are turned down simply because all the necessary information was not available or not understood. By spending some time talking about the request, you have the opportunity to provide more information and some clarity, or work through other options. The reason you have been declined may be out of your control, for example, bills that went unpaid because you moved and the company didn't change your address as you asked them to; the banker needs to know these reasons. Sometimes, things show up on your personal credit report (see discussion later in this chapter) that you were not aware of, that you forgot about, that you disputed, and that need attention. At the very least, they need an explanation. The best thing you can do is get information from your banker and the credit bureau that you can act on, correcting the record if there are errors and providing more information where it's needed.

> "No" just might mean "We don't have enough information" or "We don't understand."

The Stress of Debt

Being in debt is stressful. Along with all the other responsibilities of running a small business, you have the added worry of being sure you can make the payments on money you borrowed. By planning ahead, you can lessen the worry and sleep better at night.

When you lie awake at night because you know you have to pay your employees and suppliers the next day and are relying on your best customer's cheque to be in the mail, that's stress. As with any problem that makes you toss and turn, talk to someone. You may think you shouldn't be confiding in your banker about money worries; you may take the attitude that only good news should be shared. But in many cases, if you had involved your banker earlier rather than later, you could be sound asleep. Sometimes it's just enough to share your worries, but when you share them with someone who's on your side and knows you and your business well, that person may come up with some creative ideas. At the very least, he will provide a good sounding board, and that may be all you need.

You remember that old saying about saving for a rainy day—it still works! It's especially important to save for that rainy day if your business is cyclical. Sometimes business cycles are more predictable than the weather, so if you're running a small business in, say, a tourism-related business such as a small hotel, you're a bit ahead of the game already. You know that your peak periods are in summer, with spring and fall being slower but sustainable. The winter is the rainy day you need to save for. You'll still be facing business-related expenses—preparing promotions for the next season, renovating the premises, buying new supplies—but your income will be extremely low or nonexistent. If you've set aside some money to get you through the low periods, while still keeping up payments on outstanding debts, you'll feel in control and confident that you're running your business as efficiently as possible.

By using your business plan and financial statements as a launching pad (see Chapters 4 and 10), you'll become adept at forecasting the ebbs and flows peculiar to your type of business. Understanding what money is going in and what money is going out helps you to manage your cash flow and recognize an impending money crunch. If you review your accounts receivable listing once a month, you will realize who you are counting on to pay you in time so that you can pay others on time. By doing this simple monthly exercise, you will recognize immediately that you have trouble looming. That customer you were counting on to pay you on Monday hasn't done so by the end of the day? You've got a problem you can't allow to go any farther. Talk to the customer, then talk to your banker. Don't let this relatively minor problem mushroom into a nail-biting drama. If your banker knows you're on top of the problem, she will be more inclined to work with you while you sort things out with the customer.

Bankers know that you don't have time to race to the bank every day to tell them what is going on, but a little lead time goes a long way to developing a strong relationship. Then, when a crisis does arise, your banker can go the extra mile.

E-mail is a great way to keep your banker current.

Other simple backups for crisis times are to have an operating line in place and business credit card approved and in hand. They're wonderful ways to get some "just-in-time financing." To stay stress free and for your own peace of mind, use them when you need them. And if you feel as if you're perpetually in high-stress mode, think about how long you can live and survive this way. Not only is it taxing emotionally, it's harmful to your business when you spend most of your time thinking about how to survive rather than how to grow.

The best method of dealing with the stress of debt is to plan ahead. I know that's easier said than done, but by planning for as many eventualities as you can think of, you'll be better prepared for the ones that appear to come out of nowhere. Who would ever have predicted the events of September 11, 2001? But they have had a profound effect on all of us, both personally and in our businesses. By having a contingency plan in place—even if it's only in your head—you'll be in a better position to deal with devastating events that are completely out of your control.

Personal Credit Bureau

Part of maintaining control is knowing how others view your creditworthiness. It's easy to find out what appears on your credit report, and it's valuable information to have; after all, anyone who lends you money is likely to check out your credit bureau. You want to be sure the information that appears there is accurate, and to correct any errors.

Check out your personal credit bureau at least once a year—it's free of charge when you are inquiring on your own account. You must apply for your report in writing or go to a bureau office; in either case, you must provide the following information:

- your name, including middle initials and Jr. or Sr. if appropriate
- your social insurance number (though this is optional)

- your date of birth
- your current address
- your previous address if you have moved in the last five years
- your spouse's name and social insurance number (also optional)
- photocopies of two pieces of government-issued identification, such as a passport or driver's licence that show your address and signature

Some credit bureaus may request extra information such as a copy of a recent utility bill to prove where you live. It's a good idea to provide your phone number so the bureau can get in touch with you if necessary. There should be no charge for an annual report; beyond that, there will be a small fee for each request. Two credit bureaus in Canada are Equifax Canada and Trans Union of Canada. For a monthly fee, Equifax notifies you by e-mail whenever anything untoward appears on your credit report. You should also obtain a copy of your business's commercial credit report every year. More than 3,000 suppliers contribute data—and access is free.

When you receive your credit report, take some time to read and understand it. It will show your name, social insurance number, birth date, telephone number, current address and previous addresses, your spouse's name, current and previous employers, your current and previous job descriptions. Anyone who has requested and received a copy of your credit report will be listed. Then your credit history and banking information is set out, including the current status of outstanding loans. If there are errors, contact the institutions that provided the information and request the change. Send written proof to the bureau.

You can also use Equifax and Trans Union to check out your potential customers through one of their members (banks will also do this). Just remember that you will need to have the customers' consent in writing before any credit information can be accessed.

4 The Business Plan

You might be surprised to learn that almost all businesses, large or small, have a business plan. The difference is that often small business owners don't have to write these plans down—they carry them around in their head. Why would you prepare a more formal business plan, whether you're a start-up or an established small business? What are its advantages?

- They help you identify your competition, which will lead you to thinking about how to differentiate yourself from your competition.
- They show where and how you expect to generate revenue.
- They help you identify your customers.
- They help you identify your suppliers.
- They can also outline marketing plans and pricing strategies.

> Being aware of changing times and adjusting accordingly are necessary. What worked before may not work now! Customers change, industry and business change, governments and regulations change, so adaptability and flexibility are a pre-requisite of a small business owner.
> —G. Tyler Pellegrini,
> **Exclusive Auto & Marine**

- Business plans help you identify whether you need outside financing, how much you might need, and when it would be needed.
- Finally, preparing a business plan will force you to face some tough questions to ensure your business is successful.

Your business plan, then, is not unlike a story in a newspaper. It reveals the answers to questions any good reporter tries to find—the five Ws: who, what, where, why, when. But it goes beyond that—it can also answer how. Your first attempt at drawing up a business plan may raise more questions than it answers, but that's okay. In fact, *it's a good thing!* As you revise and refine your plan, it's doing its job by making you take a long hard look at various aspects of your business.

I should be upfront and explain why I'm such a fan of the written business plan. I'm the first to admit I'm a list maker. I can't imagine how people live without them. But I also recognize that not everyone's like me! I acknowledge that others don't need them, don't like them, don't use them. It does not mean they haven't planned as well, just that they use a method that works for them. The business plan is also just as personal in the way you approach it; it isn't about what you write, about following a model; it *is* about what you think, what you're planning for the future, and what you have to do to get there.

> **Please read this chapter even if you think you don't need to! Every business needs to plan—and you might find some surprising things about your business by going through the exercise.**

A carefully prepared business plan can make an impressive presentation to a potential investor or lender if your business needs money. As you bring in members of your team, the business plan will help them with their advice to you. Best of all, it can stand as a benchmark over the years against which to measure your business. You should review it at least every year, but ideally more frequently, to measure where you are against where you wanted to be, to identify how things have changed. But remember, the business plan is merely the blueprint. It's what you do with it that turns the plan into action! Some things don't happen the way you think they will.

I'm going to leave my banker's hat on for another moment to say that when business owners stop doing the things they are best at, the "reason they went into business in the first place," they lose focus and the business often reflects that. Things start to go wrong, albeit subtly. Because the business plan is where you can think those things through, you can revisit the plan to maintain your focus when things are going well, and refocus when things could go better.

Unlike a financial statement (a snapshot of the financial state of your company at a particular point in time; see Chapter 10), your business plan will change as your business grows, contracts, and grows again, but it will contain the same fundamental elements. If you don't take time to reflect on where you have been and where you are going, you may end up spending too much time on the wrong things—you make less money, you spend more time troubleshooting, and you may not reach your personal and business goals. The business plan needs to evolve, but you don't need to rewrite it entirely; just review it to confirm you have done what you set out to do or that what you did got you where you hoped it would.

As you prepare your plan, it's not your banker you should be listening to, it's the hundreds of thousands of successful business owners who have agreed, "Fail to plan—plan to fail." They aren't saying, "Write a business plan," they are saying, "Plan!"

Who Needs the Plan?

The plan is written to help you plan your business strategy well. I'm not the first to suggest that a business plan is like a road map. It shows where you want to go and how you plan to get there. In the future, it can show how close you are to reaching your destination and whether you should change your route.

One of the most important people to benefit from the plan is you. It helps you clarify your thoughts about your business, to approach it in an organized, clear-headed way. Anyone who will be investing in your business or lending you money will be interested in your plan. In addition, that person may come up with some questions or suggestions you hadn't thought of, so don't hide the plan in a drawer. Even if you're not in search of funds, run the plan by your banker, lawyer, accountant, marketer, your significant other—each of them could have valuable and thoughtful advice for you. If you're a start-up business, it's vital that you be honest with yourself and that you listen to each of the advisers you approach.

Mentors who have guided you in the past are useful evaluators of a business plan. These people want to see you succeed, so they won't mind asking you the tough questions you might have been shying away from. With your business plan taking form, you can look at numbers and conjectures and decide how to address the issues raised. Their aim is not to try to talk you out of starting your business but to help you find ways to succeed by identifying areas that may need more attention.

Putting the Plan Together

To be most effective, the plan needs to be well thought out. With so many things on your mind, this is one of the things you might not want to commit only to memory. Don't worry about your writing abilities; there are models, called business plan writers, that take you through the process step by step. Most banks have a business plan template on their Web site, or you can buy one.

Not all traditional business plans are designed for small business, so make sure you find one that is. The plan shouldn't be too academic and shouldn't prompt you to write pages of stuff; you'll just stop doing it because the task becomes too onerous. Remember, this isn't an essay contest. You need one that's relevant, very directed, that saves you time but covers all the points. Your accountant or banker and other small business owners might be able to suggest the most appropriate model for your business. Scotiabank has a great one online at **Scotiabank.com**.

Elements in a Business Plan Writer

Here are the elements you can expect to find in a basic business plan writer:

- *A mission statement.* This is where you can outline the purpose of your company, your business philosophy, and your vision of what you want your company to become. Think about *why* you're in business when you work on this part of the plan. When you review your business plan later, ask yourself: Has anything changed? Have I got away from what I wanted to do? It is also helpful to review your personal financial goals at this time. Your business will be key to your personal success as well.
- *A history of your company.* If you've been in a business for a few years, include basic details such as when the company started, who started it, its organizational structure, and how the company has changed. If you're starting up, your business will rely on the skill sets you have honed over many years, so include information about where you have used your talents before and how they apply to this business. Your personal resumé can be part of your business plan.

- *Objectives of your business.* Your objectives should be expressed in measurable terms. Rather than "We want to be the best greenhouse operator in the province," you should say, "In our first year of business, we want to sign up three new major retailers." Other objectives could include increasing profitability, attracting new investors, or increasing staff.

Your goals should be SMART:
Specific
Measurable
Attainable
Relevant
Time measured

- *Organizational structure.* In this section, you would include the legal name and structure of the company and who the owners and employees are.
- *A description of the products and services.* Include any special features about them and how they are different from what's currently available. If you will be manufacturing the product, describe the process briefly and include any technical advantages this gives you over your competition. What kinds of guarantees or warranties will you offer your customers?
- *Overview of the industry.* Describe the size of the industry, its market segments, who the customer is, the other types of business in the industry, the trends, and the future of the industry as you see it.
- *Marketing plans.* Who are your competitors? What are their strengths and weaknesses? How will you match or better them on price, delivery, follow-through, and support? What will your competitors do when you appear on the market? Is there room for both of you? What will make customers want to buy from you? How are you going to target these customers? What price will you charge for your product or service, and how does it compare to what's currently available?

  Perhaps you're in the enviable position of supplying a product or service that no one else does. What if some other clever entrepreneur comes along to challenge you? How are you prepared to deal with competition for the first time?
- *Staffing.* Even if you have no staff and foresee no need for a change, think about your team here. Your banker, lawyer, accountant,

insurance agent, marketing consultants—are you getting value from them? You need to have people around you who do what you can't or do it better than you can and don't sit back waiting for you to direct them. You are likely to include these paid professionals in your business plan at some point, but think about the benefits they give you. Even though you may have no plans for staffing now, think to the future. Consider whether staff you might need some-day will be part-time or full-time. Will you need to hire consultants or contract workers occasionally? Many businesses forget to include marketing consultants as one of the more important com-ponents of their business. If you know you will be hiring staff, include a brief job description and information about how each person is paid—by the hour, on commission, and so on.

- *Regulations.* Will you need to apply for any special licenses or per-mits? If you are in an importing or exporting business, be sure you know the regulations you will be operating under. Are issues of patents, trademarks or copyright likely to affect your business?
- *Opportunities and Risks.* Not all business plans will ask about this, but it's a necessary topic to consider. It shows you've thought through your business from all angles, including the worst-case ones. First, are you positioned to take on new opportunities that might arise? What might they be? How can you prepare for a business downturn? A natural disaster? A sudden rise in interest rates? A strike? Even if you don't employ unionized workers, your suppliers or customers might, so a strike at their premises could affect your business.
- *Getting your business started.* If you are starting up, outline the steps you will take to get your business going—does it involve getting loans, signing agreements with suppliers, executing a promotional plan? Certain types of businesses (for example, small manufacturer, importer/exporter, agricultural business) should include details about their premises—their size and location, a real estate appraisal, why this is a good location, and other rele-vant information.

    Your selling process is an important part of getting started. Selling is part of maintaining and retaining customers, and some of your philosophy about selling will likely have been covered in your mission statement, but this gives you an opportunity to think about it on a practical level. Think about your own selling abilities: Are you good at knowing when to close a sale and, even more important, how to close a sale? Is this an activity you'd be wiser to hand over to someone else?

- *Financial plan.* Some models will take you through quite detailed financial planning, with cash flow projections, income statements, and projected net income. These are useful exercises to work through, as they will stand you in good stead when you look for funding and give you a carefully reasoned benchmark against which to measure your business in the coming months. If you feel overwhelmed by this section, sit down with your accountant, CMA, or bookkeeper and work together on the details. At the minimum, you need to show your starting-up costs—renovations to premises, rent for premises, equipment, furniture, vehicles, inventory, taxes and licences, insurance, and supplies—and your funding—the amount you are contributing either in cash or assets, loans, lines of credit, grants, and whether you need any letter of credit or letter of guarantee.

   This exercise will help you identify your key expenses, those you can control and those you can't. Fix as many costs as you can—the day-to-day things like rent. Once you have your expenses listed, monitor them in the coming weeks and months to be sure they're not changing. With so many expenses pinpointed, you can calculate the break-even point of individual costs. That way, when an expense goes above a certain point, it will be a red flag, warning that you might not be making money any more. If your fixed costs are too high, you've got to find a way to make revenues go up. This is only one of the "stories" hidden in your business plan. This financial section will be an incredibly important part of your road map, for it will show you whether you've stayed on the freeway, wandered off to the side-roads, or ended up in the wilds. And it will show you if those are better places to be than the ones you had your sights set on at the beginning!

- *References.* Provide the name and phone number of your banker, accountant, lawyer, insurance company, and marketing agency.
- *Executive summary.* This step, best performed at the end, is the one most people will see first. Keep it short (one page is best, but two pages is the absolute maximum), enthusiastic, realistic, and informative. It introduces the reader to you and your business, outlines the

highlights of the business plan (your main objectives, the marketing opportunities, your proposed schedule for getting your business off the ground, and so forth), and entices the reader to learn more about your business. Be sure to include details such as your business's name, address, and phone number, and your name, address, and phone number if they are different from the business's; don't forget e-mail addresses, too.

Contingency plans. Include a description of the contingency plans you have put in place should you fall ill, become injured, or die. You should have both disability and life insurance, especially if you have a family; sometimes a disability can cause greater financial hardship than death because of associated medical expenses. Many large corporations plan for eventualities such as the unexpected death of their top managers and executives. There's no reason you shouldn't follow their lead.

Format. Depending on who will see the business plan, you may vary the format of the presentation. By preparing the document on a computer, you can cut and paste to create abbreviated forms of the plan or to highlight different sections, just as you might do with a resumé, tailoring it to needs and interests of the reader. A summary of the financial section may suffice when you show your plan to a mentor—but your banker and accountant may also be interested in the figures.

What Your Business Plan Can Tell You

As you've been preparing your business plan, you've probably already been interpreting and analyzing the information you've been gathering. But once you've completed the document, have another look at it. Many business owners are surprised to find that the plan contains surprising information when it is looked at as a whole. If you're a start-up and this is your first business plan, you might find

- you don't need to borrow as much money as you thought you did, and you can save money by borrowing only what you need. Borrowing too much can take away from your diligence in containing your expenses. You could also be led to believe that your company is doing better than it is.

- you have too few suppliers—if one leaves the market, you'll be in serious trouble.
- there are components of your business you don't enjoy, say, paperwork, and there is no one in place to fill the gap.
- you have more—or less—competition than you thought.
- you have more to offer than your competitors and you can charge more for your services.

An established business might find that

- it's time to change the ownership structure.
- although your customer base is growing, you're losing old customers—it is more expensive to attract and bring new customers onside than it is to service existing customers. This is a warning that something could be wrong.
- you have new competition.
- there are opportunities to expand your business beyond your current market.
- it's time to get your business on-line to attract new customers from new markets.
- your expenses have increased over the past five years, but your prices don't reflect the change, so you're not making as much money as you used to.
- you have too much inventory.

Of course, each owner is going to find different information and look for opportunities or flashing lights or red flags that signal trouble. You may discover that it's time for a change, or that things are better than previously thought. But all business owners should share a common interest in reviewing their business plan, updating it, revising it. If you're growing quickly, visit it more frequently. Remember that it is the vehicle by which you think through your business.

5 The Winner's Circle

Surround yourself with winners. Although many people who start small businesses are independent minded, many of them quickly recognize that they can't do it all themselves. In fact, it's rare to find a business owner who has the ability and capacity to do it all. Calling on those who have expertise in areas that confuse you, puzzle you, or just plain bore you is a wise move. Some of these people will become part of your team for the life of your business, and others may be there only during certain phases.

Who are the main players likely to be? You'll recall from Chapter 1 that I mentioned a banker, lawyer, accountant, bookkeeper, marketer, and personal financial planner. You'll find that many businesses don't involve anyone else. Whoever they are, though, they should understand your dreams and goals. It's a two-way street: you listen to them, but they should also listen to you. Tell them about where your business operates from, who your customers are, the history of your company so far and the background of the business you're in. Tell them who your suppliers are. Your suppliers, too, are part of the web of relationships you're setting up. And then there are your customers. Without them, your business has no purpose.

> The biggest obstacles I faced were those placed in my path by my own fears. As a 26-year-old female with five part-time jobs and my father's old car as my only asset, it was extremely difficult to get financing. I learned to question everyone: accountants, bankers, lawyers. If the answer didn't make sense, I simply found a professional with sensible answers. This meant telling a lot of people "no" and believing in myself.
> —Julie Anderson, Your Dollars Store with More, Blairmore, Alberta

For help in finding or replacing a lawyer, accountant, or bookkeeper, talk to other small business owners, your banker, friends, and family members. Before long, you'll have set up a useful network of connections. It always impresses me how effective small business owners are at networking!

As with all dealings, at first meetings clarify what hourly rate the professional charges, outline the services you need, and ascertain how experienced the person is. Don't forget to check out the professional associations or societies that can direct you to the specialists in your geographic region; you can find lists of associations in directories at your local library or by searching in the Internet.

Bankers

As mentioned earlier, everyone needs a bank even if it's only to provide a place for you to deposit and withdraw money. Even at that very basic level, though, the bank offers another valuable service by providing a record of all the financial transactions you do through its offices. It provides a handy record of your receipts and expenses in much the same way your credit card bill does.

About 50% of small businesses borrow money from a bank either by conventional business loans, credit cards, using equity in their house, or various other ways available to them (see Chapter 3). Even if you're like the many small business owners who never fill out a loan application form, your relationship with your banker should be for the long term and should be a mutually rewarding one. As I stressed in the preceding chapter there is a lot more a banker can do for you than just lend money.

Most small businesses use a bank to conduct their financial affairs. They like to know there's someone there with whom they have a relationship.

One of the great time savers for the small business owner is the ability to bank through your computer or over the phone. When you're shopping for the right banker and the right bank, visit their Web sites to assess what they offer. This will give you a good basis to start your discussion of your needs.

Finally, confidentiality is vital. It leads to trust. As I said before, your banker can share with you what he's learned in his experiences dealing and working with other small businesses, but this advice must be general so as not to give away "trade" secrets—including yours.

Lawyers

Next on your shopping list might be your lawyer. You're going to be running a business, so, if possible, look for someone who specializes and understands small business. The friendly lawyer down on Main Street who drew up your will may not be the appropriate professional for your particular business. Apply some of the same standards you applied when you chose your banker: make sure she has a passion for understanding small business and is interested in providing current knowledge on issues that concern small business owners.

Here are some of the things a lawyer can help you with:

- drawing up the documentation required for your business
- informing you of zoning bylaws and any other local legal restrictions
- helping you draw up contracts with landlords, suppliers, customers, and others with whom you do business
- making patent searches and applications
- pointing out potential areas for liability

Accountants

Accountants deal with business records and other business-related financial matters. You've already come across references to accountants in earlier chapters, especially in the previous chapter on the business plan, but it might not be clear that their services often differ from those of a bookkeeper. Large accounting firms may also supply bookkeeping services, but because your bookkeeping may be simple, you may not need someone with specialized expertise.

Here are some of the things an accountant can help you with:

- preparing your business plan (see Chapter 4)
- setting up a system for tracking revenues and expenses
- offering financial advice, including matters concerning taxes (for example, what are the tax implications of the business structure the lawyer has advised?)
- choosing the correct type of business structure
- preparing your financial statements and explaining them to you
- preparing income tax returns and helping you with other reporting required by the government

There are three types of professional accountants:

- Chartered Accountant (CA): who specialize in taxation, develop financial reports for external users (such as bankers and investors), prepare financial forecasts, and undertake external auditing. They are sometimes involved in wider issues than financial ones.
- Certified Management Accountant (CMA): who specialize in developing internal information about the cost of your product or service, information that assists you in decision-making. They can be involved in a wide variety of tasks: monitoring and analyzing every aspect of a company, including planning, sales and marketing, human resources, finance, and so on.
- Certified General Accountant (CGA): who specialize in financial accounting, external auditing, and taxation matters for small businesses.

As you can see, accountants are much more than glorified bookkeepers. They may be involved in every aspect of a business. If you are simply looking for someone to keep your financial books in order and up to date, a bookkeeper will be cheaper and more suited to your needs (see below).

Your accountant can help you find ways to increase cash in your business by improving your inventory management. For example, they may find something languishing at the back of your warehouse that you could get rid of, thus freeing up the space for something that sells faster and that will give you some cash. Not to say that you couldn't find it as well—it just may be a matter of finding the time!

Bookkeepers

When a small business hires or contracts a bookkeeper on a part-time basis, it's a great example of small businesses working together. Large firms often employ their own bookkeepers, but many bookkeepers are self-employed, just like you, selling their services to those who don't need a full-time, in-house bookkeeper.

Here are some of the things a bookkeeper can help you with:

- prepare your accounts, and check and balance them
- enter your daily financial transactions in a journal (frequently on computer)

- maintain general ledgers and ensure they balance
- prepare draft financial statements for your accountant to save time and money
- prepare various reports—statistical, financial, accounting
- collect your accounts receivable. Many business owners prefer to have someone else undertake this key role so that they can spend their time managing the relationship with the customer without having to undertake the "Hector the Collector" function as well.

If you're confident in your own ability to do your own books, buy a computer program and do them yourself.
Advantage: **You'll benefit by knowing intimately how your business is doing.**
Disadvantage: **You might be able to spend your time in a more fruitful way.**

Insurance Agents

As a small business owner, choosing an insurance agent should be part of the financial planning you do for your business, as well as for your personal life. It's all about contingency planning. Again, talk to other small business owners and your banker for advice on finding a reliable, knowledgeable agent. Talk to the agent about which types of coverage you need. The following are some of the most common for small businesses:

- *Personal liability:* protects you against claims made by anyone who suffers a bodily injury on your premises
- *Fire:* will allow you to rebuild or repair your premises and replace lost or damaged equipment and inventory
- *Automobile:* covers your car while it's used for the business
- *Disability:* provides income if you cannot work because of illness or injury
- *Life:* provides protection for your beneficiaries in the event of your death
- *Business interruption:* compensates you for earnings you lose if your business is halted due to a natural disaster such as flood, fire, tornado, ice storm, and so forth
- *Crime or theft:* reimburses you for losses caused by theft or employee dishonesty

- *Product liability:* protects against lawsuits if customers are harmed by your product
- *Bonding:* ensures that a party in a contract will fulfil their part of the deal or protects a business owner from an employee's wrongful conduct
- *Creditor life insurance:* pays out the balance on your outstanding loans in the event of your death

Suppliers

Your suppliers are vital to the success of your business. You need reliable sources for the materials you require to produce the goods and services you sell—*all* your suppliers need to be reliable and trustworthy.

It's quite likely you're setting up a business you know something about already, so approaching suppliers may not be a problem. But now that you're starting out on your own, it's worth the time to check out the competitors of the suppliers you know about. You may find yourself balancing the reliability and higher prices of suppliers you know against the lower prices and unfamiliarity of a new supplier. Only you can decide the value of the various elements you will consider when making these choices.

You're obviously going to have many more relationships than those outlined above: there are your customers, for example (see Chapter 6); office staff and warehouse staff (see Chapter 7); and people who work for you on contract—Web designers, sales representatives, marketing firms, advertising agencies, and consultants. All these people are important and are likely to become members of your team when professionals such as your banker, lawyer, and accountant are being chosen. With everyone who's going to be on your team, you're looking for the same thing: someone who fits with your personality, someone who will be interested in what you are trying to accomplish, someone who has integrity and honesty and is optimistic.

Marketing

The marketing aspect of your business is as important as the other aspects, yet it's often forgotten. This might occur because people are confused about what marketing actually is. Dictionaries define marketing as the action, process, or business of promoting, buying, and selling products and includes market research and advertising—in short, getting the product from the producer to the consumer. Most businesses might make the definition more restrictive, and define it to mean publicity, advertising, and promotion, as well making your products available and getting them into your customers' hands. But by hiring a marketing company to work with you, your ideas might undergo some changes. Some of the items a marketing consultant will be qualified to advise you on include

- the packaging and bundling of your product
- what kinds of sales outlets your product should appear in
- the price you're asking for the product
- the type of service you will provide
- researching your intended market
- how to reach your customers by advertising (the promotion of your product)
- how to research your competition
- whether surveys and focus groups are appropriate to your product or service
- how to address social changes brought about by changing demographics, interests, values, and so forth, that can affect the sale of your product or service

Remember the four P's of successful marketing:
the right Product
the right Price
the right Place
and the right Promotion

And don't forget WIFM—that's what's top of your customer's mind: What's in it for me. Look at things from the customer's point of view and emphasize what's in it for them.

Some small business owners love the part of their business where they present the public image of their company, take advantage of free publicity, even create opportunities for free publicity. Others aren't as comfortable doing this. Fortunately, many small companies, similar to yours, are in business to do your marketing for you or help you draw up the right marketing plan. Understanding your customer, your target market, and your market opportunities, whether local or global, is key to the success of any business. You may need someone to help you understand the most effective way to get to that market and acquire business from it. Marketing experts know how to do this more quickly and more effectively than most business owners. And although you also have expertise in this field, consider buying some time from that marketing expert. It's amazing what another perspective can open up.

For some good ideas on how to promote your business, go to www.cbsc.org/osbw/promo.html.

Business owners need to find experts who are interested in their business, their personal goals, and their business goals, and who are sincerely interested in helping business owners succeed at those goals on their terms. Like Julie Anderson at the beginning of the chapter, learn to say no to those who don't give you the support you need. This doesn't mean you're looking for yes-men; you're looking for people who respect your ideas and can help you with their specialized knowledge. Since you know what it is you want to accomplish, keep looking until you find associates with the right attitude for your business, as well as for your personal aspirations.

6 Managing Your Business

You've assembled your team, you have your finances in order, including suppliers and customers. You've done your business plan! Life is good. Money is coming in and it's going out. Your customers are happy, and your customer base is growing. You have a little time to examine how you can make your business more efficient, how you can save money, and whether it's time to expand your customer base. It might be the time to move on to a new business or retire altogether. You might also be considering whether hiring staff on a full-time or part-time basis is appropriate; I'll talk more about hiring staff in Chapter 7, and in Chapter 11, I'll discuss issues connected to retirement, selling, or winding down. But now we're going to focus on particular ways to manage your business, no matter the type of business you're in.

Your Customers

Every business needs a customer—someone who wants to buy what you're selling. You probably already know who your customers are likely to be, in a general way, at least. In some rare cases, such as when you have a brand-new idea or product, you'll need to do market research to find your customers and use marketing techniques to reach them.

Once you've got your customers, don't take them for granted. Take time to think about them. Who are they? How did you acquire them? How have you managed to keep them? What is it about your repeat customers that keeps them coming back? Can you do more of that? It's cheaper to keep the customers you have than to acquire new ones. Determine if there are ways to enhance your relationships with your existing customers to get more business from them. When you review your customer list, do you see opportunities to sell more products or services, improve your efficiencies, and maximize your time with your customers?

Set a "service promise" to your customers that provides value to the customer. Know how your service or product will benefit the customer and communicate it regularly.

Customers look for five key benefits when they are making the decision to buy. What you're selling will

- save them time. Will the product save them time, or will the service you're providing make them more efficient in their use of time?
- save them money. Your product or service may be less expensive than your competitors' or it will allow your customer to spend time more effectively elsewhere.
- provide the best-quality product or service.
- offer the customer peace of mind because your business has integrity and provides top-quality service.
- make them feel good. Some customers purchase services or products for prestige and recognition; whether it's because your product or service is the best there is, it makes them feel special.

Knowing your customers is important. For example, if you are the owner of a shop selling CD players and have a customer who is motivated by ease of use, don't bring out a copy of the manual for her to read. She wants to know that she can dim the lights, lower the volume, and be the hit of the party with a simple push of the button. The next customer may be looking for top quality and will pay the price for it. You show this customer the specific details that make the product the best quality.

Find out what's important to your customers by asking questions. Involve them in conversations as you involve the other members of your team. As you learn more about your customers, you can hone your message for each different circumstance, as illustrated in the CD player example above.

Identifying your customers' needs is even more important than what your product can do—that part comes later. If you think speed is what's important to your customer but the customer knows flexibility is, you're going to be missing the mark. When you listen to your customer and discover that flexibility is important, that's what you promote to that customer—speed becomes an added value to your customer but not the most important thing.

Stay focused on the main message, the one that's important to your customer, and don't oversell. Where customers are concerned, there are three words to remember: Listen, listen, and listen.

> **You've got two ears and one mouth for a reason—when you are selling you need to listen twice as much as you talk!**

Selling is part of maintaining and retaining customers relationships. One of the hardest parts of selling is closing the deal even when you hear that the customer is ready to buy. Learn to listen for sales opportunities. It's an art to know when to say, "Would that work for you?," "Shall I start the paperwork?," or "Can I write that up for you?" Not all of us are born knowing how to sell, but most of us can learn. Others find it easier to hire someone else to do it. Take a course or read a book, but make sure you know how to "sell" your business!

Once you have a happy customer, work to keep her happy! Maximize your opportunities with existing customers; it's more efficient than finding and getting to know new customers. Be sure each customer is getting everything from you that your business can provide. Don't overlook any chance to provide more value to your customer. I've been impressed with my hairdresser's suggestion that I book my next appointment as I leave his shop. This makes life easier for me and guarantees he'll see me in three weeks rather than four or five when I get around to calling him. He's made my life easier in an unobtrusive and thoughtful way. It doesn't even seem like selling. By maximizing the business you already have in your "yard," you can sometimes get twice as much benefit from one customer.

When you get a new customer, assume this person will be staying with you for the life of your business. And then work to make it happen! Know your customer. Set the terms under which you hope to do business. Communication is all-important. Be clear about what you need and what you, in turn, can do. And because this is a business you're running, you need to make sure the new customer will be able to pay you for the goods or services you're providing. This is especially important when you put credit terms in place for the customer. Most banks can provide you with a basic credit report (see Chapter 3) at minimal cost; it tells you if the customer's credit rating is satisfactory but not a lot more. You can also request information on other businesses through the Better Business Bureau or Equifax.

Your Cash Flow

What do people mean when they talk about cash flow? They're referring to the cash you have to keep your business running day to day. Managing cash flow well is absolutely vital to the well-being of your company. In fact, poor cash flow management is one of the major reasons for business failure. Your business can live without ever making a profit, but it cannot live without cash flowing in.

> **Cash flow is the amount of money available to you on a daily basis to run your company.**

Don't let great sales figures mislead you into thinking that your business is in good shape. Your sales may be skyrocketing, but if your customers aren't paying you for 60 or 90 days, or even 120, you may have trouble making payment on your own bills that need to paid within 30 or 60 days. This is one of the most dramatic illustrations of cash flow problems. Everything feels fine until you realize you don't have enough cash to pay your bills. If you find yourself in this kind of squeeze, you need to make some adjustments to improve your business practices and help your business operate more efficiently. Consider the following:

- *Look at your inventory.* The value of just-in-time inventory control cannot be overstated. The more inventory you stockpile in your business, the more cash you have tied up. If the inventory sits around for too long, it ends up costing you money, especially if you borrowed to acquire it in the first place. Review your inventory on a regular basis, and determine if some items are just taking up shelf space. Ask yourself if you are better off selling them at a reduced price than holding on to them for a long time. And don't fool yourself into thinking things "will come back in style." Obsolete inventory is usually just that—obsolete. Best of all, to manage your inventory, set terms with your suppliers that match the length of time you expect to have and sell the finished product or inventory. Nothing feels better than to collect cash from your customer on a sale for inventory that you have not yet had to pay for.

- *Look at your ordering practices,* which are closely related to inventory control. Just-in-time ordering can save you a large outlay of cash for large orders, especially when your supplier can guarantee delivery within a week. Carrying only what you need will help keep cash in the bank to pay immediate expenses. Large orders should be considered only when you are cash rich or can get a good discount for the purchase. If you borrow to make the volume discount purchase, do the math. Does the amount of interest you pay on the financing cost you more than you are saving on the discount?

- *Look at your accounts receivable* to ensure your customers are paying you on time. I know this sounds simple, but it is one of the most challenging components of running a business. You make the sale, and then, the honeymoon is over—you have to collect the payment from your customer. If you can't get cash upfront, you may decide to establish the terms of repayment with your cus-tomer. Congratulations! You have just become a bank for your customer! Every time your customers leave your business with their goods or services on credit, you have lent them money.

- *Look at your accounts payable terms.* Could you extend the payment date? Instead of paying them cash in 30 to 60 days, they may accept payment in 60 to 90 days. Each time you negotiate this way, you improve your cash flow management.

If your business has a greater ebb and flow than can be addressed by the simple remedies described above, you may want to talk to your banker about an operating line (line of credit). This allows you to draw on it in times of need, knowing that when you get paid for that big contract, you can repay the operating line and have enough cash on hand to maintain a balanced cash flow for some time (see Chapter 3 for more about operating lines).

> **To improve cash flow, collect what you're owed quickly and pay what you owe on the day it is due.**

Planning Your Cash Flow

Because your cash flow is such an important part of your business, you'll want to know how to plan around it.

Controlling Cash Flow

Set the expectations up front. Make sure both you and your customers understand the rules you'll operate by. When do you expect payment? Will you send them an invoice?

Keep good records. Every time you extend credit to a customer, keep a record of when the invoice was made and when it is due. I've had people write the list of who owes them money while they're sitting at my desk, only to realize they had a $5,000 account receivable they had completely forgotten about. By recognizing how long the invoice has been outstanding, you can determine how you want to do business with this customer the next time. If you have customers who pay regularly and on time, you know you can count on their money on time in the future. The longer you wait for money from your customers, the harder it will be to collect it, and the less you will want to do it. Who wants to try to build up a long-term customer relationship with someone you have to call every week for your payment?

If you aren't good at it, find someone who is. Not everyone is good at collecting money. Even some bankers hate calling their customers to ask for late payments. But you deserve to get paid for the work you do. If you're spending a lot of time collecting your payments, hire someone to do the collecting for you.

Know when you'll need cash:
- Is it predictable?
- Do you always need certain supplies at certain times?

If it's not very predictable, you'll need to be sure you always have some easily available cash for those times. If you can identify cycles in your business, you'll be able to predict when you should be especially vigilant about being paid on time.

Have a plan of action in place for when you need cash from other sources. This is especially important if you have an unpredictable cash flow. Know where you can get short-term money: Will it be on your credit card, from your operating line, or your personal savings? Perhaps you have a supplier who will allow you to extend your payment for another month. Keep a good relationship with these sources. When times are good, keep your credit card payments up to date; if things get tough, let the people you owe know what's happening.

Depending on how closely you need to control your cash flow, you might do cash flow projections monthly, even weekly. There's no better way to head off danger than paying attention to the cash that's coming in and going out of your business. You'll quickly see if you have an important payment coming up and know whether you need to get some money in the bank to cover that payment or negotiate other payments in the short term. You might be tearing your hair out, trying to satisfy customers, making calls on them, attempting to drum up new business, and watching the crucial cash flow figures. When it all seems too much, stop, take a deep breath, and become your own consultant. Review what you do best. If it's not overseeing the cash flow problem, seriously consider bringing in a bookkeeper who can help even just for the critical period you're in. If you see that you need someone full-time to do this, or another aspect of your work you don't like doing much, consider hiring full-time staff. You might consider investing in one of the many software programs available that could help you with your accounting and cash flow planning. Look for programs that will help you with accounts receivable and accounts payable management, and where needed, your inventory. Even if you hire a bookkeeper to use the software, you should review the reports regularly and use them as a management tool for your business finances.

Advantages to controlling cash flow   There are many advantages to controlling your cash flow and planning for its ups and downs, for knowing when money comes in and goes out:

- At its most basic, cash flow planning tells you where your cash is going. If you're in the fortunate position of having excess cash and you have a good overview of your future cash flow, you may be able to set aside some of the excess cash to grow your business or invest outside your business. Neither is a bad idea!
- You can plan for your short-term cash needs. If your business goes through natural highs and lows, you may be able to foresee when you will need to borrow some short-term money and plan for when it will be paid back. Those you borrow from need to understand how and when you will pay it back, ensuring they will be happy to do business with you again.
- When you decide you need to borrow in the short term, understanding your cash flow will help you decide the type of financing you need. You can forestall an emergency by knowing that January,

for example, is always a slow month or a month that has many payments coming due. Knowing this means you can prepare for it. Some businesses use credit cards to cover this type of short-term debt because it can be interest-free money. Almost all credit cards have a grace period that allows your balance to be interest-free if paid off within the required time frame—usually 21 to 26 days from the statement date.

- You can control when you should make new purchases, when you should replace, repair, or overhaul outdated or aging equipment. If you purchase a piece of equipment in order to do a specialized job for a client, you could consider financing it to match the revenue stream it will create. In other words, rather than paying for the equipment out of your operating line, take out a loan that can be paid back in monthly instalments. These monthly instalments are, in effect, financed by the increase in income the equipment generates, and if you don't expect that to happen, you might think twice before agreeing to go ahead with the purchase.

- In a seasonal business, such as ski hill operator, you'll have a good income for several months, but your expenses may continue all year. Being in control of your cash flow means you won't overspend in the good seasons, leaving yourself short in the off-season.

- A bank might ask to see your cash flow projections when your business is growing or if you need additional financing. If you keep it updated and under review, you'll always be ready for this request. In addition, banks will sometimes lend you money based on your accounts receivable, especially those with 30- to 60-day payment dates. Take a report of your accounts receivable with you if you're going to see your banker about a short-term loan. Your banker may also look at the larger picture to help you determine if you have a short-term cash shortage or if your business is in need of something more permanent, like a cash injection or some term financing.

Understanding and planning your cash flow is vital for a new or growing business; for a mature business, it can help you see whether your business is thriving or stagnating. Use this as an opportunity to put new life back in your business. Just remember that a lack of profits won't kill a business as quickly as poor cash flow. You can eke out a relatively unprofitable business for a long time as long as the cash flow isn't interrupted. Yes, it's easy to lose track of the coming and going of money when you have so many other aspects of the business to consider, but without a healthy, predictable cash flow, you'll soon have no business at all.

How to Plan Your Cash Flow

Preparing a cash flow statement is not unlike preparing a budget and balancing your chequebook all at the same time.

All businesses have income that arrives in a variety of forms—cash, cheque, or credit. You need to estimate when it's going to come in and then when those cheques and credit card receipts are going to show up in your bank account as cash. The other half of this equation is knowing whether that's likely to happen in time to meet your loan payment, your rent commitment, salaries to your staff or subcontractors.

Drawing up a cash flow statement is relatively easy. Start with a period of six months, since it's often easier to project over this shorter period than a whole year. Estimate your monthly sales, based either on your past experience or your educated projections. Look at payments due to you from your customers. If you've been in business for a while, you'll have some past figures to go on, but if you're starting up, prepare a projected cash flow to identify how your customers will pay you, to determine what expenses you have to pay, and how much cash you need to have to carry you through until your customers start paying you. It's safer not to be too optimistic. If you expect income from other sources, such as interest from bank accounts or investments, add that as a separate entry. Calculate your total income for each month; this is called your total receipts.

Now move on to your expenses. What are you going to have to buy each month? What are your operating expenses? Do you have staff to pay and office, factory, or warehouse overhead to include? Don't forget a separate entry for taxes. For your own interest and to be sure you've thought of everything, you can make this section as detailed as you want. You might want to make separate entries for insurance, fees, repairs and maintenance. Add up these totals for each month and you have what are called disbursements.

Subtract your disbursements from your total receipts to see what your cash flow is for each month, positive or negative. As a final step, enter your beginning cash balance and add your net cash receipts or subtract your net cash disbursements. In an easy-to-read and easy-to-understand chart you

A Sample Cash Flow

Cash Receipts	1st Month	2nd Month	3rd Month	...	12th Month	Total
Cash Sales						
Collection of Accounts Receivable						
Load Proceeds						
Other Cash Receipts						
Total Cash Receipts **A**						

Cash Disbursements						
Purchase of Materials or Stock						
Purchase of Fixed Assets						
Accounting and Legal Fees						
Advertising						
Vehicle Expense and Travel						
Business Tax, Fees, Licences						
Property Tax						
Management Salaries						
Other Salaries and Wages						
Employee Benefits						
Rent						
Insurance						
Interest and Bank Charges						
Payment on Loans/Mortages						
Maintenance and Repairs						
Freight						
Telephone						
Utilities						
Office Expenses and Postage						
All Other Operating Expenses						
Income Tax Payments						
Total Cash Paid Out **B**						

Cash Surplus or (Deficit) (A–B)						
Opening Cash Balance **C**						
Closing Cash Balance **D**						

*Note: Line "C" is a carry-forward from line "D" in the previous month.

have a projected picture of the cash flow of your business over the next six months. Use this information in conjunction with your business plan to make changes to your business and to monitor what actually happens every month.

Credit Investigations

Your customers expect good and reliable service from you, and the products and services you stand behind. They trust you to deliver what you say you will when you said you would and at the price quoted. In return, you expect to be paid in a timely fashion. But what if you're dealing with extending credit to customers who are new to you? As a responsible business owner, it is only prudent that you carry out a background check to assure yourself of their creditworthiness. Not every customer will need a credit check, and the level of checking may vary with the customer, depending on factors such as how much business you expect to do and how long the business has been established. If your customers pay cash or use a debit card or credit card, you don't need to bother with a credit check. You have access to their cash right away.

> You can do a credit check through the Credit Bureau, Dun & Bradstreet, or the Better Business Bureau (refer to the Appendix for contact information).

Collection Procedures

If you're like many business owners, the responsibility of making sure you're paid the money you're owed will fall directly on your shoulders. This can be one of the most difficult tasks facing a small business owner. It's a hard decision whether to spend time trying to collect on outstanding debts or to drum up new business from people who may pay more quickly. But at some point—and it's better earlier than later—you have to make every attempt to collect the money owed to you.

When you first recognize a payment is past due, contact the customer and in a friendly, firm, and tactful way discuss the problem; have all the information at hand regarding the account. Negotiate terms that are acceptable to you and set clear deadlines, but also be prepared to issue warnings—perhaps you will need to stop filling that customer's orders until the debt is paid. It's important to be courteous and civil throughout the conversation, as this is likely someone you want to continue doing business with. When you've agreed to terms, it's advisable to follow up with a written note of the phone call to be sure there is no room for misunderstanding. Note in your calendar the date the payment or first instalment is to be made, and if it is not made, follow up immediately to see why your agreement has not been honoured. At this point, you have to decide how long you want to continue the negotiations. When you feel you've exhausted all your options, you may decide to talk to a collection agency.

For a fee, usually a percentage of what is collected, a collection agency will attempt to collect what's owing to you. Their fee or commission will vary depending on the amount they are collecting and can range from 10% to as much as 50%. Only you can decide what it's worth to you, but don't forget: often something is better than nothing. Choose a reputable collection agency—both the Credit Bureau and Dun & Bradstreet offer collection services. You can also check in your Yellow Pages. A call to your local Better Business Bureau, or a visit to their Web site, will advise you if any complaints have been made against the company that owes you money. Other business owners or your banker may have recommendations as well.

Minimizing Tax

If this is your first business, you'll find some differences in your income tax preparation. One similarity, though, is that you have to pay it! Another similarity is that you still need to keep track of expenses and income. You'll become even more interested in finding ways to reduce the tax you pay. There is nothing illegal about attempting to minimize your taxes, but the complexities and frequently changing rules of the system make it difficult for the busy small business owner to keep on top of the best strategies for doing so. This is where a relationship with an accountant really pays off. Your accountant's business is to stay abreast of changes to the regulations, and if she is part of your team, you can expect her to keep you fully informed of changes that affect you and your business.

One question that often arises as people embark on their new business is whether to lease or buy premises, cars, equipment, and other expensive items. There can be tax advantages to leasing: depending on the type of lease you take, the payments can be expensed to the business, lowering your income and ultimately reducing the amount you pay tax on.

Other tax-minimizing strategies include the following:

- Consider putting the maximum allowable into your RRSP every year; in addition, talk to your accountant about the advantages of income splitting with a spousal RRSP to lessen your taxable income when you start drawing the money out.
- Talk to your accountant or lawyer about the advantages of incorporating (see Chapter 2). Companies that are deemed to be small businesses under the Federal Income Tax Act pay a reduced rate

of tax compared to large corporations. But be sure to look at the idea from all angles, not merely the tax-minimizing one.

• If you set up your office in your home, you can claim a portion of all house-related expenses—mortgage interest, rent, utilities, and other expenses—as business expenses. The percentage you claim should reflect the relative amount of space you use; if your office and business-related space is a fifth of your total house or apartment, you can claim a fifth of your house-related expenses.

A Hard Truth

Sometimes the business plan and cash flow statement, as well as your natural feel for your business, tell a story you'd rather not read. A declining market brings you face-to-face with some hard questions. You may need to make some radical changes and difficult decisions to continue your business's success. Laying off employees may save your business, but it doesn't make it any easier.

Some businesses have a natural life cycle. If you think you can revive it with some financial help and can make a good case for its continued existence, take this information to your banker or other trusted adviser. Remember, by now you have a banker who truly wants you and your business to succeed. Let your banker help you look for options to help you do just that. Know whether you're looking for short-term money to get you out of temporary difficulties, or if you're looking for help over the longer term to make more fundamental changes to the way you run your company.

One of the most important thing to know is if you're making or losing money. If your business is growing so fast you are losing customers, you need to understand the implications. Don't be afraid to talk to your banker about this; it is one of the most important times to keep all your relationships strong. It is understandable to be concerned about how the bank will react, but if you've been diligent about maintaining contact with your banker over the good and bad years, you'll have a lot of credibility, and your banker will be looking forward to working out an action plan with you. During a downturn in the business cycle, either of the economy generally or perhaps your particular industry, you might need to reduce prices for a while or cut costs in some way.

This is a good time to go back to your business plan—it's your anchor in both good times and bad. Use it to analyze what's happening. The next chapter focuses on the pros and cons and how-tos of hiring staff and keeping them happy.

7 Hiring Staff

Some small businesses tick away quite happily for years without employees. The owners contract out the jobs they don't like—bookkeeping or marketing, perhaps—or the jobs it doesn't make sense for them to do—warehousing or selling. But the day may come when your voice mailbox has more messages than you can cope with, the fax machine has spewed out enough paper to carpet the hall several times over, and there's so much e-mail, it doesn't bear looking at. On top of that, a supplier hasn't delivered the vital component you need to fill an order for your biggest customer, because you forgot to sign and return a purchase order. You haven't had a holiday for three years and your spouse is giving you the silent treatment. Life is chaos! It's time—way past time, from the sounds of it—to hire an employee. It sounds scary, but it doesn't have to be.

To Hire or Not to Hire ...

First of all, you might not need a full-time employee. Hiring an efficient person might be the answer, and even working part-time, this individual could keep most of the chaos at bay, leaving you to select the most important matters to deal with and delegating the rest. "Delegate" can be one of the most difficult words for the self-employed to utter, but once you've given it a try, you'll wonder how you survived before. You may find that hiring one person full-time to do what different contractors have been doing for your enterprise can save money and result in a better-organized business.

In Chapter 5, I talked about what various people can do to help you, so once you've made the decision to take on that bookkeeper, sales rep, or office assistant, there are some other decisions to be made. Will that person be full- or part-time? Work in your office or from her own office? What are the implications for your business of hiring staff?

As you go through the process of deciding whether or not to hire, don't think of the salary of the new person alone. There may be added costs to having an employee: you may need such things as a new desk, a new phone, a cell phone, and a new computer. There will be additional responsibilities (see below) inherent in becoming an employer. Once you have an idea of the costs and effects of being an employer, will that new employee, directly or indirectly, help you increase your sales or efficiency or somehow save you enough money to cover the salary (and other expenses) you project? What if your figures show that you only break even on the deal? It's still probably worth it, because having someone help you could allow you to see more customers, pursue new customers, investigate changes in your industry, and spend more time with your family. Not all benefits can be measured by the bottom line, but some of them end up improving the bottom line, even when that wasn't your main purpose.

The Responsible Employer

When you become an employer, you assume a number of responsibilities. You need a business number that identifies your company. You will be responsible for ensuring that your employee has a social insurance number. You will need to deduct income tax, Canada Pension Plan payments, and Employment Insurance from your employee's salary and pay those amounts to the government regularly. When you withhold tax from your employee's pay, you're holding it in trust for the government. The money is not calculated as part of the income of your business; if you were to go bankrupt, the government would be entitled to get what you owe it ahead of any other creditors. Here's what you need to know and where to get information.

- Contact your provincial Ministry of Labour to obtain free guides on becoming an employer. Ask for a copy of the current employment standards act and its guide. The act outlines things such as minimum wage, hours of work, overtime, deductions, vacations and statutory holidays, severance pay, pay equity, and termination. Knowing the details is important, so if you're tempted to skip over them, sit down with your lawyer for an hour or two. Some industries are regulated by the federal government, as well; you can get information about the standards by going to the Web site of the Canada Business Services Centres: **www.cbsc.org/ osbw/employer.html**, click on Employment Standards, then click on Federal. This Web site will also connect you to sites with information about some of the topics in the rest of this list.

- Get an Employer's Kit from your local Canada Customs and Revenue Agency (CCRA) office. When you make the request, you will be given an employer number that you must use when you send any records or correspondence to CCRA. The kit includes a booklet to help you get started; tax exemption forms; tables that show how much income tax, Canada Pension Plan contributions, and Employment Insurance you should deduct from your employee's pay; a remittance form for your first report and payment (thereafter you will be sent a form on a monthly basis); and a guide about the records to be completed in the case of termination.

- Check with the Workers' Compensation Board (WCB) to see if you are one of the industries that must pay a fee to the board.

- Familiarize yourself with human rights legislation, both provincial and federal. There are clear prohibitions against discriminating on the basis of nationality, citizenship, race, colour, ancestry, age, sex, marital status, pregnancy, religious or political beliefs, mental or physical disability, or criminal convictions. Even though you may be employing only one person, these laws apply to you every bit as much as they do to large corporations.

- Be prepared to keep careful records of your employee's name, address, birth date, social insurance number, number of dependents, date of employment (and termination), occupation, the number of hours worked every day, the wage rate and when the worker was paid, the deductions you've made, and vacations and statutory holidays your employee has taken off. These records will be used to calculate your employee's wages, and the information must be sent to CCRA when you send in your payment for the deductions and when you fill in T4 summaries for your employee. Human Resources Development Canada (HRDC) also needs these records in the case of termination to calculate employment benefits.

Finding the Right Person for Your Business

A written job description will make it clear to candidates what it is you're looking for and what the job entails. A job description may sound unnecessary for a one-person office, but it's better to be safe than sorry, and it doesn't have to be fancy, just functional. If there is any dispute over the terms of employment, or miscommunication about what is expected from the employee, it's good to have a written job description to fall back on. In the job description, include an overview of the duties and the skills needed to perform those duties. Add any special information about hours or working conditions; if you think you'll need someone for only a specified period of time, say so. If you'll be expecting an employee to work late occasionally or to work weekends as needed, be sure to include this in the information. Decide what qualities are important to the job and which skills or qualities would be a bonus. By being specific and detailed, your expectations will be set clearly, and interested candidates can do a bit of self-selecting. If you need an employee to work evenings and weekends those who cannot need not apply. You don't have to go through the exercise of interviewing a potentially good candidate only to find at the end of the interview that the person cannot put in the needed hours.

Use the job description to be clear in your own mind what you expect this person to do. Then create a classified advertisement based on the job description, choosing the main items and adding the conditions that are important to you. You could be swamped with applications from inappropriate candidates if you are too vague. Remember the human rights legislation when you draft this ad, and specify that candidates will be tested if you intend to do that. Run the ad in your local paper or that of a nearby city or town. You can decide how you want the candidates to contact you—by phone, mail, fax, or e-mail. In a tight job market, you might be willing to advertise your phone number and take calls directly. In a looser job market, you might ask for resumés only and not advertise your phone number. Newspapers offer the service of providing a box number at a small extra charge, and will hold and forward all applications to you. If you give out your phone number, be prepared to deal with the phone calls that are bound to come in. It's acceptable to say in your ad that only candidates who will be interviewed will be contacted; this way, you don't have to get in touch with each person who applied. Study some ads in the paper you're likely to use to get an idea of what works and what doesn't.

You can also find potential candidates by contacting local high schools and colleges; personnel agencies sometimes specialize in particular types of business (look in the Yellow Pages under Personnel Consultants) and can be a good source of part-time help. In addition, HRDC can help by matching your needs with suitable registrants in their files. Then there's good old word of mouth—ask around. Rely on that network you've been nurturing. Other business owners, friends, family, your accountant, your lawyer, your marketing consultant, all of them know people who would be suited to your business;

it can be especially fruitful when they know what your business does, and what you need. Think about how you're likely to reach the candidates you want to attract. Consider advertising in journals, magazines, and papers aimed at a specific group of people: women, ethnic groups, or specific industries such as engineering, nursing, or teaching. There are also a few Internet sites that allow you to post your job on-line. An excellent example is **www.pleaseapply.com**, which helps local businesses locate employment talent. You want to attract the widest pool of candidates and make your short-list selection from that.

The Interview

From the applications you've received, narrow down your choices to the best four or five. It can be tempting to interview everyone, but you can end up confusing one applicant with another. If you're not happy with the selection in that first group, rethink your ad. Perhaps it needs to be revised to attract the kind of candidate you're interested in. Spending this extra time and money will be worth it in the long run.

Before the interview, prepare a list of questions you want to ask each candidate and know what you expect to elicit from your questions. If you've never been in the position of interviewing someone, practise with a friend or family member. It won't be exactly the same as a real interview situation, but it may point out some weak spots you can work on. Rehearsing can also highlight weak or poorly worded questions. In addition, by keeping the same questions for each candidate, you get a better picture of who best meets your requirements.

Word your questions so that they cannot be answered with a simple yes or no. You want to get the candidate talking. Try not to let the interview veer into areas other than those involved with the job. Without intending to, you may find yourself discussing issues that are prohibited by human rights legislation. Even something as innocuous as discussing where a person was born could be construed as prejudicial. In addition, if you plan to have a probation period, include that information in the interview. Probation periods—usually three months—give you and the new employee a chance to get to know each other. You can observe how well the person takes direction, whether the new hire is able to work independently, and whether the two of you are meshing. It's easier to terminate the employment by the end of the probation period than to allow a problem to go on. If your gut tells you there's something wrong, it may be best to let the person go during the probation period, as the reasons for termination are not as stringent as those that apply after the probation period.

Conduct the interview in a relaxed atmosphere. Don't answer your phone; switch it over to voice mail during the interview. Let the candidate know you intend to take notes during the interview, but avoid such comments as "man about 50" or "woman with small kids" or "young man in wheelchair." Such comments might help you differentiate between the various candidates as you review your notes, but they could be grounds for a charge of discrimination. Your notes will help you know who is right for your job. Allow at least half an hour for each interview and give yourself some time between interviews to make notes. Don't overload yourself by trying to interview everyone in one day.

Hiring is a two-way process—you and your business are being judged too! If you normally wear jeans in your office, don't haul out your business suit for this occasion. You'll be looking for skills and experience in the candidates, but how you and the interviewee interact and connect is also important. If you're casual and laid-back, you'll want someone who's comfortable in that atmosphere.

In the end, make sure you listen to your instincts. The combination of good interviewing and good instincts are a recipe for hiring success.

Hiring the Successful Candidate

Once you've assessed the candidates and settled on the successful one, check the references you've been provided with. Inform the candidates that you will be checking their references. When you call for the reference, confirm the dates the person worked and the positions held. Because former employers are concerned about privacy, most will not give you any information beyond this, but you can also ask about work habits, how the candidate got along with others, whether the candidate was responsible. It's a good idea to keep a record of these reference checks.

Once you're satisfied with the chosen candidate's references and there are no outstanding questions in your mind, you can offer the job to the candidate. It's always best to find a way to do this in person. If you have to do this over the phone, it's best to follow up the offer with a letter to confirm details such as job title, salary, and starting date. Keep your records with the thought in mind that if something goes wrong, you have evidence that you did everything properly. Once your employee starts working for you, however, treat her as if you expect everything to go right. After all, you made this hiring decision and are likely willing to stand behind it completely.

Working with Your Employee

Even if your new employee has worked in your field before, you might have some practices that are different from other workplaces' practices. Take the time to go over how you work—or how you'd like to work!—and remember that your employee can't read your mind—yet. Once you're used to working together, you'll both likely have a good idea of how the other thinks, but that takes time.

> Hire people who can do the job better than you can. Surround yourself with the best, and you will be the best.

You may need to practise delegating; it's sometimes hard to give up all the things you've been used to doing, especially if you like doing them or think you do them better than anyone else. Don't forget that you hired this person to help you, so take advantage of his experience, knowledge, and willingness. If you hire correctly, you will soon be able to trust your employee to do the job better than you. Give him the opportunity to learn on the job, as well. If your office is just the two of you, it's a great atmosphere in which to share decision-making. You've got someone on the spot you can bounce ideas off; you'll soon discover if your employee brings a fresh and interesting viewpoint to your discussion. Remember, though, most employees will not have the same dedication, commitment, and interest in your business as you do. You live, eat, breathe, and dream about your business. Your employee probably goes home at the end of the day to concern himself with other matters. This does not mean he's a bad employee!

Even though you're a small company, you should have a formal policy about when pay increases will occur and whether they are tied to performance. Even in small offices, talking about salaries can be difficult and an employee who doesn't know when her next review is due may hesitate to bring up the issue and become concerned that her work isn't valued. Rather than approaching you, she may even start looking for work elsewhere. You've spent valuable time and money on your employee and you don't want to see her walk out the door.

Scheduling performance reviews and talking about pay increases means that there is a set time for you and your employee to talk formally about how things are going once or twice a year. Even though you may ask every few days, "How are things going?," it's difficult for someone to answer honestly as you breeze by to look at the latest sales figures.

If the person you've hired is working right in your office, rather than being on the road as a sales rep, for example, he could become the linchpin of your business. Now you have someone who can tend the office while you go on holiday or travel on business. There are a number of questions you should ask yourself in this case: Will he be able to sign cheques in your absence? How far will his responsibilities extend? What if you were to become ill for several months? Could this person run your business on a temporary basis? These are all issues to be discussed with your employee as you assess his capabilities; talk the situation over with your banker, too.

Terminating an Employee

No one likes having to let an employee go, but it happens. Sometimes your business simply can't support the extra person any more. Often this type of termination doesn't come as a surprise to the employee; he's likely seen a slump in orders and knows what that means. Perhaps your attempts to deal with performance problems have failed.

Never go straight to the bottom line when you're thinking of termination for substandard performance. Identify the problem and work with the employee to try to correct it by an agreed-upon date. Document these attempts in case the employee can't turn things around. If the employee does respond positively to your suggestions and his performance improves, be sure to recognize this. If the employee hasn't made a change, however, you'll have no choice but to terminate his employment. This is never easy. It's painful for both of you and emotions frequently run high. You may experience regret, anger, and relief at the thought of the termination, and the employee may well feel the same emotions, though at a higher pitch. Ultimately, you have to do what is right for your business.

It is helpful, and could save you a great deal of money in the future, to first talk to a lawyer experienced in the field of labour law to be sure you've done everything legally required of you; she can advise you of any legislation affecting termination that you should keep in mind. You can dismiss an employee for "just cause," which includes such things as insolent behaviour, wilful neglect of duty, theft, and intoxication.

Once you know clearly what the grounds for dismissal are, inform the employee privately. Keep your emotions under control and be respectful of the employee. Get to the point quickly and make it clear when you expect the employee to leave. It's often best to pay the employee for the period of notice and request that he leave the next day. Keeping him around after he knows he's leaving can be detrimental to your business, your customer service, and your other employees. Be respectful to all of them. The workplace is unlikely to be a happy place while the dismissed employee works out his notice.

Being an employer may sound like a lot of work, but many small business owners look back gratefully to the day their prized employee walked in to the office. It gave them time to attend to the business of their business rather than the office details, or it allowed them to deal with customers while someone else negotiated with suppliers. Perhaps it just let them have a day off every week. Or it freed them up to take their business to another level, which is the topic of the next chapter.

8 Growing Your Business

Growing your business to the next level may have been part of your plan from the day you first started your business. On the other hand, your company's growth might have taken you by surprise and you find yourself wondering whether you want to take it to what appears to be the next logical level. How do you now when it's time to grow? And what does growing your business mean?

When people talk about "growing their business," it usually means they want to expand it by selling a new product or increasing their sales, their staff, and their premises; they may want to move into markets or countries they haven't done business with yet. In those early days, when you were starting your business, you wanted to get enough sales to support your business and yourself. Now, just as you did then, you may see an opportunity, but it means you need to grow to take advantage of it. Or you suddenly realize your business has got there before you, which is a sure sign that you're putting in longer hours, working harder to keep up, and beginning to think something needs to change. And that's the key, whether it's a planned growth or an unexpected and happy surprise: something is going to need to change if your business is going to grow effectively.

A word of caution: before you jump on the "bigger is better" bandwagon, take a good look at what has made you successful at getting to this point.

Perhaps your success is because you can practise economies of scale; this usually means that big companies can be more efficient and economical than small companies can because the large companies can devote workers to one particular task at which they are skilled rather than having workers doing more than one task. In your case, perhaps it's your small size that allows you to provide a service or produce goods that a larger business would find prohibitive. If that's true, growing may not be in your best interests.

Take some time to weigh the pros and cons. What might you have to sacrifice to grow? You'll need to take into account that increasing sales in a growing business doesn't necessarily mean a bigger figure in your bottom line right away. Once you've assessed the likely effect on you, your business, your family, and your life outside your business, you'll be in a good position to make an informed decision about whether to keep your business at its current level or jump into a larger pond, whether it's expanding into the next city, your whole province, all of Canada, or the world.

Let's look at the areas that will be affected by your growth.

Personal Growth

Let's start with the most important person—you, the owner of the business. When you take a hard look at what you are about to undertake, are you prepared physically, mentally, and intellectually to meet the challenge of a growing business? You really need to ask this question first, because all the rest are follow-ups. Remember why you wanted to be a business owner in the first place. Does this growth fit into your personal plans? If your business grows by 20%, will you have to put in 20% more time? Is that physically possible? What does your significant other think? What do your children think? Are they prepared to see less of you, certainly in the short term, as you take this exciting and challenging step?

You will require new and different skills to manage a growing business and may need to grow beyond what you've always been good at. You may need to improve your financial knowledge in order to operate successfully, and your management and leadership skills as you increase your staff and motivate them with your vision. Are there courses you could or should take to help you in this area?

Take a look at where you are in your own life. You're obviously someone who likes being in control, and likes a good challenge; that's why you are successful as a business owner. But your life situation may have changed or you might have reached the goals you set and feel satisfied with the way things are. You also probably recognize the way your heart beats a bit faster when you think of expanding, of reaching new markets, of growing. Is that increased heartbeat because of fear or the thrill of a new challenge? Be aware of the difference between that instinct to go out and conquer new markets and the part of you that says, "Things are fine the way they are."

You'll give yourself different answers at different times of your life. You're not a failure for deciding this isn't for you right now!

Your Customers

Looking at your current customers, are there any conclusions you can draw from what you know about them that will provide a basis for reaching more customers or a new market? How can that information get you more business? You may need to undertake new research to help you effectively market to your new customers and you may need to turn to outside help in this area. How easy will it be to get your products to your new customers? Can you maintain your current level of good service?

You can't take for granted that your potential customers are the same as the ones you've always served, especially if you are expanding into a new country. It's important to know whether there are cultural differences that will affect your ability to do business, from the type of customer who will be interested in your product or service, to the way business is approached in a different culture. Even simple things can make the difference between successful and not.

Then there's the issue of customer service and how it will be affected by the changes in your business. You pride yourself on the customer service you deliver, personal service that creates repeat business and loyalty. As you hire more staff, you must depend on others to create that very same customer experience that you have based your business on and that has become your image and your promise. You will need to work hard to avoid having the growing of your business conflict with maintaining your service commitment. Handling the gap that often occurs when a business grows is one of the greatest challenges. You don't want any valued customers falling into that gap—that time when your business is in a state of flux as new employees are taken on board, new systems are set up, and new suppliers are being tested.

Your Market

As you contemplate these issues involved in growing, don't forget to look at the market space your business is thriving in. Is it big enough to accommodate your growth and to maintain it for the long term? Will you need to grow outside your current markets to make your business bigger? Have you researched those markets sufficiently to know that the opportunity exists? Do you need to go outside your community, your province, or even your country to seek the right opportunities to grow? What do you know about your customer in this new market? Who will you be competing against in the new market? How will you deliver? Are there any additional costs? Will you need to understand new complexities for your business: exporting, importing, travel, Internet, and e-commerce sales opportunities?

If you're thinking of going outside the Canadian market, expanding into the United States has many advantages. For example, you can benefit from the favourable foreign exchange rates. You may feel you're selling at a premium but in U.S. dollars your product or service may seem like such a bargain you can sell them for more than you can in Canada. Mexico is another country that offers wonderful business opportunities for Canadian businesses. With the North American Free Trade Agreement (NAFTA) in place and government agencies available to help ease your way, the attractiveness of moving into these markets is greater than ever. Know why your being a Canadian business is an advantage to your new customers. Perhaps the standards in Canada that apply to your business are higher than those in the new country you're entering and this is an advantage to you. For example, Canadian safety standards for children's toys mean that people in other countries buying these Canadian-made products will know these toys do not present a hazard to their children.

> **Be sure the bank you deal with is represented in the countries you're expanding into. It makes it easier to transfer funds.**

In order to enter a market in a new country, you may have to engage an agency to represent you, although you may instead decide to be even bolder and just move your head office there. There's no doubt a reputable agent on the spot is a good short-term solution until you see what the prospects are. Licensing, taxation, and duties are all issues you need to investigate when doing business in another country.

Finance and Capital

You'll need to determine what impact the new sales opportunities will have on your expenses and your bottom line. Revisit your business plan, your projections, and your last financial statement and look at what will change financially. Work through a break-even scenario to see how much new business you need to pay for the new equipment, the new employees, the new office space. Where can you improve efficiencies and use your knowledge and experience to make your expansion into another market or country as efficient as possible?

Don't forget to talk to your banker. Keep her apprised of your progress because there are so many things the bank can help you with—letters of credit and letters of guarantee, just to name a couple. Because of its connections in many countries, a bank can facilitate the movement of money coming in and going out. Since the tragic events of September 11, 2001, many businesses are increasing their use of banks to manage the moving of money from Canada to other countries. With renewed focus on anti–money-laundering legislation, not only in Canada but in many countries around the world, it just makes it easier to get money where you need it to be. You may need to set up a new support system or add to your current one—lawyer, accountant, marketing expert, sales team, especially if you're doing business in a new country.

Your Suppliers

You're not in this alone. If your business is growing, other businesses will be growing too—your suppliers' businesses. You need to know that they can keep up with your new demands as you increase your customer base and support you as you expand your reach into other markets. This is a place you can look to help you manage your cash flow. If the size or frequency of your orders will be increasing, work to negotiate a better discount or more preferential credit terms. You may need a backup plan in case your normally reliable suppliers can't cope with the increase in business you're sending their way.

Human Resources and Leadership

As you start to grow, you will likely continue to spread yourself thinner and thinner until you find you need additional employees. What is the role you should play in this larger business? Will you need to contract out some of the administrative work or hire staff to allow you to focus on the job of growing the business? What are the roles you need to fill and what skills will any new employees need? Do you need people with specialized knowledge and, if so, are they available? Is your business planning to employ your spouse or children?

If you've been able to run your business with no employees, making the leap to becoming an employer at the same time you're expanding into new markets could raise your stress levels to heights you've not experienced!

Part of your time as an employer will be spent dealing with performance issues and developing your staff to grow as your company grows. In addition, you may find it's desirable to incorporate (see Chapter 2), which will change the structure of your company.

Leadership

The issue of leadership is closely related to human resources, but because it's so important, I've separated it into its own category. Are you a leader? Think about the implications. You already are a doer—you wouldn't be contemplating this exciting new move if you weren't. But when you have employees, it's not just enough to be a doer, you must also be a leader. Will others follow your lead? Can you motivate them? Do you want to? Many business owners like the fact that they are in total control and answer to no one. This will change when you hire your first employee. You now have someone who is relying on you to guide and inspire. It sounds contradictory, but leadership means answering to everyone, not just your customer and yourself, but to those who work for your business as well. You will need to articulate to your new employees where you want your business to be, how you are going to take it there, and what role they will play. Your communication skills will be key.

Information Technology

As you grow, you will need to review your business structure, your reporting methods, and the way your paperwork is prepared. To look after this expansion, new technology may be necessary, whether it's increased hardware capacity or the purchase of new software, such as a new accounting program to reflect the increasing complexity of your business or a program that helps to monitor work in progress or goods shipped. Make sure these costs are accounted for in your financial projections. It's not a given that anything has to change, but thinking it through gives you peace of mind and removes any surprise costs that might show up along the way.

Marketing

Effective marketing can help you increase your business and sustain its growth. Choose the methods you will use to tell people you're growing and examine whether you need to change your marketing strategy to reach new customers. What will it cost, and what will you get in return? Like everything else you'll be looking at as you assess your growth, assess its cost-effectiveness, at least over the longer term.

Don't forget what you learned earlier about marketing: be sure to emphasize what the benefits of your growth are, both for your current customers and your new ones. If you're moving into a new market, you need to be able to measure the effectiveness of your campaign. In order to assess whether you're reaching your target, for example, use coupons that customers need to redeem or return. This is market tracking at its most basic, but it works. What works in a big city might not have the same impact in rural Canada or in Mexico. Remember the four p's of marketing: the right product at the right price with the right promotion in the right place.

Sales

Growing your business may mean that you have to change the way you sell to your customers. Word of mouth may have worked well when your sales area was contained geographically, but it won't be enough in a new and larger market. Your current ability to hustle may not be enough to keep you moving forward. You know by now whether selling is your strength. If it isn't but you've been doing okay up to now, the gap could become more obvious. Perhaps you or your staff need specific skill training and specific strategies to set goals and work to reach those sales targets. Ensure that you have the right people in the right jobs. Choose sales staff and service staff who are relationship builders, then put the support structure in place to handle the increased sales activities. If you don't, your service may break down, your after-sales service may falter, and customer loyalty and repeat business will be at risk.

You may need to have a separate sales force in your new market, especially if it's in a new country. Do you hire people familiar with the new market or do you use an agent to sell for you? While you would prefer to find someone with both those skills, it may be a difficult task. But by approaching this challenge the way you've approached your other business challenges—carefully thinking through your business plan, talking to reliable associates—you'll make your decision based on the best information and advice available.

So here you are—back at the business plan, asking yourself the same old questions, but in a completely new light. Try some "what if" scenarios in your business plan. See what happens to your numbers when you think about growing. You may find that bigger isn't always better. How can that be? If you need to add people, increase space, and buy new equipment, you might actually make less money than you are today. Even if it "looks" like more money, the effort might not be worth it. What you want to see is an incremental growth that provides for a bigger bottom line with less effort. In the short term, you might have to burn the candles at both ends, but over time, you should be able to see the benefits of the work.

Taking your business to the next level of growth is not always as challenging as it sounds; in fact, it can be a lot of fun and offer many rewards. Your experience as a business owner, your expertise in your area of business, and your desire for success are the key factors that help you make your decisions. My job as a banker is always to make sure that the tough questions get asked and to help you think through your business plan. And you're not alone when it comes time to make the big decision. As I've emphasized throughout the book, use your team of colleagues who understand you and your business—your banker, your accountant, your lawyer, your marketer. Seek counsel from your friends or family and your trusted mentors. Then make your decision, and go!

9 Your Internet Business

How did we survive before the Internet? Even people who a few years ago didn't own a computer, much less know how to turn it on, are happily sending e-mails around the globe, ordering their groceries from a Web site, and "surfing the Net" as a form of entertainment. Any business that doesn't get on-line to some extent stands a chance of being left behind. Small business owners, fortunately, tend to be what's called "early adopters." They're interested in anything that will make their business better, that will help them cut costs and time, that will let them reach their customers more easily and expand their customer base. So, generally, they're at the head of the line when new technology hits the market.

Your computer contains the life of your business: correspondence and record keeping for orders and personnel and financial matters. You use the computer to access the Internet to do your banking, research, selling, and promotion. In fact, many run a business that exists only on the Internet. The Internet is ideal for small business owners, but has some challenges, too. First, let's look at what it can do for you.

Improving Efficiency

The Internet can improve efficiency in many ways:

- Researching on-line saves time. You can find out what your competition, locally and around the world, is doing. You can also seek out new suppliers and research new markets. The best thing is that the Internet never closes its doors—it's open when you're ready to use it.

- Banking on-line rather than standing in line to use a banking machine saves time. You can make your bill payments, transfer money between accounts, and check balances. You can see up-to-the minute information about what cheques have cleared and which customers have paid directly to your account, so it's a fast and easy part of managing your cash flow. The variety of transactions you can undertake on-line has increased tremendously in a short time and is likely to increase. You can pay your taxes on-line, check out your investments, correspond with your broker, and manage your investments. All banks in Canada have Web sites that spell out what's available.

- E-mail correspondence between you and your customers is a great way to keep in touch—no more telephone tag. You'll find that long-distance charges go down significantly when you start relying on e-mail. And you'll have an easy-to-track record of correspondence in the case of misunderstandings or disputes.

- Doing business on-line is efficient and economical. You can place orders late at night and know they'll be read in the morning, and you can easily advise customers that their order has been sent.

Research

Many business owners use the Internet to do research—to find out about products, competitors, suppliers, taxation matters, how to hire an employee—everything from what affects their business to what is happening in general in the business world. The Internet can improve knowledge in areas that are important to them.

The Internet is a huge asset in research because it can take you places you'd never get to otherwise, and you can go when it suits you. Over forty percent of small business owners use the Internet to order supplies, transfer money, and manage their cash flow.

When you surf the Net, you'll find out who your competitors are not only down the street but across the world, too. You'll be able to pick up ideas from around the world. Imitation is not only flattery but good business, too.

Almost 25% of all business owners use the Internet to increase their knowledge, train, and upgrade their education. The big attraction is access of information when it suits you and not when a college or other educational institution tells you to. One course of interest to small business owners can be found at **www.vusme.org**. Check the Appendix for more Web sites to help in your research.

Getting On-line

Even if you're not interested in doing business over the Web, you should seriously consider getting a Web site for your business. It's a great way of letting your potential customers know you exist. You'll receive all kinds of advice about building your own Web site, everything from your next-door neighbour recommending his brother to suggestions about hiring a professional Web site designer, to doing it yourself. For a couple of hundred dollars, you can get your business set up on the Web. For a quick and easy way to get on the Web, check out Microsoft's bCentral (**www.bcentral.com/**), software designed for small businesses; it includes components for e-commerce, e-mail marketing, finance, appointment scheduling, and more. For less than $500 initially and $35 a month you can be up and running quickly. The advantages to using it to set up your Web page or Web storefront are that all the bugs have been taken out, and that it will consider the basics of Web design: how much copy should appear on a page, how and where the buttons and links are positioned, and much more.

Brochureware. One way to establish your business on-line is to have a site that acts like your business brochure. It gives information about what you do, and what you offer, and, most importantly, how to reach you by phone, by e-mail, or at your store or office. Your customers can't buy your products from these information pages, although software is available that will transform your original information page into a site where people can actually order. For many businesses, this is the latest step in dealing with their customers. It's vital, though, that the page stay current and up to date.

The way your Web pages look is important, and as you put them together, keep in mind what you want your site to do.

- Who are you trying to reach?
- Is there anything restrictive that shuts out potential customers?
- Is it easy for customers from other countries to order your product?
- Is there a converter for different currencies?
- Is it better to show all prices in U.S. funds and accept payment in those funds?
- What is your returns policy?

Before you launch your Web site by adding your Web address (URL) to your business cards and letterhead or displaying it in big bold letters on your delivery vans, ask some customers whose opinion you value to do a test run of your site. People like them will be using the site, and you want it to be effective. If visitors can't read the text, can't figure out where to click, or can't get to a page they want to, they won't stay long and they may never come back. You may discover that the way you list your products or set up your order page is not useful to the customer (it might be useful to you, but that's not the point!).

Service Industries. If you're selling services, set up your site so that you can suggest to potential clients other services they might need. If you're a lawyer, for example, and someone visits your site to get information about drawing up a will, you can add links to other pages you've prepared that cover related issues, such as estate planning and insurance. You'll be providing potential clients with more valuable information that will reflect well on your business.

Some businesses even provide links to their competitors' sites! They do this because they have a particular niche, either in price or special interest, and know they're not losing business by directing site visitors to merchants who deal in cheaper or more expensive goods. For example, a guitar store in Toronto provides links to guitar dealers who specialize in high-end guitars, something this store doesn't deal in.

Use your Web site to do surveys to find out what your customers, or potential customers, really want from your business. Testimonials on the page from satisfied customers will give your business credibility.

Your Web site may be the cheapest employee you'll ever have.

Support. Using the Internet can reduce overhead, save you time, and make more money. If you're in a different geographic area than most of your customers, the Internet is a great way to reach them. And whether you use the Internet only for e-mail or to do your banking or for all your business, it's worth having a local "tech guy" who becomes your computer guru. Talk to other computer users who use their computers in much the same way you do. If you are not tech-savvy and have no interest in being so, you may need someone who will do house calls to fix problems and help install new software and equipment, keep you updated on new virus checkers, and generally be thinking about you and your needs. The technical support person has got a finger on the pulse of what's happening in the computer world and you're running your business—together you should make a formidable team.

How Will People Find You?

How are people going to find you in the great unregulated universe of the Internet? Through search engines—Web sites that index millions of Web sites, such as AltaVista and Google. A Web directory performs a similar function; it arranges sites by category so that they are easily found by browsers. Some Web directories are LookSmart, Open Directory, and Yahoo!

To get listed by the search engines and directories, you have to list your site with each of them. The Web site of each search engine or directory will have complete instructions. The process can take anything from a few weeks to a few months, so plan ahead.

People will also find you if you can link your site to other people's sites—your suppliers, customers, and organizations or associations that have some relevance to your business. Ask if you can provide links to their pages from your site and ask them if they will do the same for you. Gradually, you'll build up an e-network, similar to the one you've formed with other business contacts and advisers.

Getting Ready for Business

In order to do business on the Web, you need some way of collecting money. You can always resort to the "cheque in the mail" routine, of course, but that seems to negate the advantages of doing business on the Internet.

In Chapter 2, I described how to obtain a merchant account, which lets you handle credit card transactions, so let's expand that to the Web. First, talk to your banker, who needs to know that you will be doing credit card transactions on-line.

Be prepared to pay a slightly higher merchant discount rate because you won't have a signed transaction slip. In the future, this drawback will be overcome—that's how important doing business on the Web has become.

The bank will want you to confirm that your site has clear information about how to contact you, what your returns policy is, your shipping charges—information that any credible on-line business would post as a matter of course.

Ten Tips to Success on the Web

1. Don't make your home page (the first page) a mystery. Make it informative—who you are and what you do should be clear. Put your name, address, and logo on every page of your site. If possible, make the logo the link back to the home page.

2. Make it easy to find your phone number so people can call you. A toll-free number is a good investment if you're going on the Web.

3. If your site is large—more than 50 pages—provide the ability to search the site.

4. Be straightforward. Keep your language simple and user friendly. Not everyone understands the lingo of your business and industry; write to the lowest common denominator to attract the most customer prospects. Make the titles and headlines tell the story clearly of what the page contains.

5. Make the pages easy to read so that people accessing the site can quickly scan them. Use lots of space. Don't clutter up the page. Group information using bold words and headings.

6. Avoid long scrolling pages; only 10% of people go beyond what they see on the screen. Keep the best content at the top of the page. Instead of cramming it all onto one page, use links to structure the content so readers can get the detail they need quickly.

7. Invite people to e-mail you, but set the response area so their messages can be a maximum number of words. You don't want to be inundated with lots of long messages.

8. Underpromise and overdeliver. Put a message on the Web site that you'll respond to e-mails in 48 or 72 hours. Then get back to them within 24 or 48 hours—you'll look good.

9. Keep your site current. You'll lose the ability to attract repeat visitors if your information is out of date or inaccurate.

10. If any part of your site takes longer than 10 seconds to load, you'll lose visitors. That's the maximum time people will wait for a page to download. When you have your site tested by friends, ask them to check how long they have to wait for the site to fully load.

In the past, some people have had difficulty getting their merchant accounts for doing business on the Internet, but as these transactions become more common and security continues to improve, we will see even more transactions done this way and it should become easier to be approved. One reason is that there is no imprint of a card when you accept it on-line or customer signature to the intent to pay. On-line signatures are not far off, however, so this problem will soon become a thing of the past. Setting up your site to accept credit card payments will save you administration and collection time.

Running Your Business On-line

The Web will provide an adjunct to your existing business; that is, to broaden your reach, bring in new customers, and be a source of new suppliers. But for some people, the only business they have is the one they run on the Web. They don't have a storefront or office, they don't sell in any other way. Starting a Web-only business is more difficult than moving an established business to the Web. As you probably know, just about anyone can set up a Web page and proclaim themselves to be in business. Your potential customer needs to know that you're trustworthy and that you'll provide what you say you will. This can be a difficult hurdle to overcome.

Link your site to others. Look for partners whose business complements yours. A small country hotel could link its site to a local car rental agency or to the sites of local museums, stores, or the regional tourist association.

Offer discounts to people who visit your site then use your services or buy your products. Provide a coupon on-line that can be printed by the customer to bring or send to your store or office. This will help track where your customers are coming from and signal whether your site is generating business. And of course, e-mails from customers are a measure of interest. Some on-line stores purposely don't display prices, partly to encourage the interested customer to send an e-mail and partly because the price of what they're selling is negotiable.

The Web is a great way to manage customer service. These days it's much more likely that someone will send an e-mail to ask questions or order than pick up the phone to do the same. You must be vigilant in answering the e-mail that comes in. Set up an automatic response to let your correspondent know that the e-mail was received and when you will respond. Be sure to respond in a timely fashion—real-time questions expect real-time responses.

The Web-only business faces extra challenges. You're relying on the Web as your only medium to reach your customer, unless you also decide to advertise elsewhere. But advertising can be expensive, unless you know how to reach your targeted market, whoever they may be. You also need to know that the people you are trying to reach are people who use the Internet. As more and more people get on-line, the opportunities increase. If you're in the process of moving your business on-line or doing part of your business on-line, don't get seduced into spending hours exploring the Web, adding more bells and whistles to your site. Remember, just keep it simple.

Security

Security on the Web is less of an issue than it used to be. Nevertheless, you need to be able to assure your customers that their information is safe. The information to be safeguarded is not only credit card numbers, but also personal or confidential information regarding the business they do with you. Talk to your tech expert, who can advise you of the latest developments in making your transactions safe and secure. Beyond that, familiarize yourself with the risks. Many of your customers will express concerns and will need reassurance that your site is as safe as the latest technology can make it. Be sure whoever is setting up your Web site (if it's someone other than you) is reliable, knowledgeable, and experienced. If you've created your own Web site for selling because you don't want to pay an expert to do it, at least be prepared to pay a consulting fee for a Web design service to see if they can hack—or break—into it. This will be money well spent to demonstrate to your customers that you've implemented safety measures. Create a separate page on your Web site detailing the software installed and the steps you've taken to make their information secure. When you use a recognized security program, you will receive the upgrades as they are released.

The area of technology that concerns itself with protecting Internet transactions changes rapidly and is always improving. By the time you read this book, specific information could well be outdated, but the important thing is that you're aware you can benefit by taking your business on-line.

The Future

Doing business on the Internet will continue to expand. Businesses are already paying their suppliers on-line, just as they can accept credit card payments from their customers on-line. Already, businesses are able to receive notices from their bank on their cell phones to tell them when a deposit has been made to their account, or a large withdrawal has cleared. These innovations are just another reason to stay in touch with your banker, so that as new e-commerce services are available, you can decide if they are useful for you and your business.

10 Financial Statements

Chapter 4 discussed the importance of having a solid business plan. You also need to find a good way to measure your success—you want to know if your plans, and your actions, did what you expected them to do. Measuring your success can be done in many ways—through rating customer satisfaction, employee satisfaction, and your personal satisfaction. You can measure it by the increase in customers your business shows. You can measure it by how much money your business makes for you. Your financial statements are another tool to help you ascertain whether you are doing the right things for you and for your customers.

How often you prepare your statements is really up to you, but you need to do it at least once a year. In fact, every time you or your bookkeeper puts an entry into your ledger, you are working on a part of your financial statement. At the end of the business day or the business year you can see the picture made by these individual entries and understand their cumulative effects. You know what you want your business to do for you, and the statements will show if it is really happening! In the end, though, the important question about financial statements is not how often should you look at them, but why?

First, though, let's look at the advantages to keeping good records:

1. They can help you identify the sources of your income.
2. They can save you money, including tax savings.
3. They can help you recognize where you are losing opportunity or losing money.
4. They can act as a tool to help keep you better informed about your business.
5. They can help you get loans from the banks and other creditors, including family and angel investors (see Chapter 3).

Business Structure and Tax Reporting

Before I go on to describe financial statements in more detail, I want to review the position of each kind of business structure (see also Chapter 2) with regard to taxes.

Sole Proprietor

- As a sole proprietor you have to register for GST/HST (harmonized sales tax) if your worldwide taxable income is greater than $30,000 (see Chapter 2 for information on how to apply for your GST number).
- A sole proprietor pays taxes by reporting income (or loss) on a personal income tax and benefit return (T1). The income or loss forms part of the sole proprietor's overall income for the year. Part of your income tax return will include the form "Statement of Business Activities." This statement is a proxy for the profit and loss of the business.
- As a sole proprietor you may have to pay your income tax by instalments.
- You can file your tax return no later than April 30 every year, though small businesses can wait until June 15 to file. Tax payable balances are due at the end of April. If you pay later, you will pay interest.

Partnerships

- A partnership, by itself, does not pay income tax and does not file an annual income tax return. Each partner includes a share of the partnership income (or loss) on a personal, corporate or trust income tax return, depending on who forms the partnership.
- Each partner has to file financial statements at tax time. You need to do this whether you receive your share in the form of money or in credit to your partnerships' capital account.
- A partnership must have a GST/HST number and file a GST/HST return, remitting tax as necessary.
- You may need to remit income tax instalments quarterly or annually.
- The date for filing the partnership's tax return depends on the type of partnership you have. Check with your accountant.

GST/HST Reporting Periods

Annual taxable revenues at or less than $500,000	Annually
Annual taxable revenues $501,000 to $6,000,000	Quarterly
Over $6 million	Monthly

Corporations

- As a single entity, a corporation has to pay tax on its income and therefore must file its own income tax return.
- It must also register for the GST/HST if its taxable worldwide annual revenues are more than $30,000.
- A corporation must file a corporation income tax return (T2) within six months of the end of every fiscal year even if it doesn't owe taxes. It has to attach complete financial statements and the required schedules.
- A corporation pays its taxes in monthly instalments; your accountant can advise you regarding the filing date and whether installments are required.
- Corporations have reporting periods for GST/HST, at which time they must file a return.

Anatomy of a Financial Statement

A set of financial statements generally consists of four elements:

1. a balance sheet
2. an income statement
3. a statement of cash flows
4. a statement of retained earnings

I'm going to focus on the first and second.

The Balance Sheet

The balance sheet tells you what your business owns, what the business owes, and whether the difference is positive or negative. In other words, it shows your net worth, or your equity in the business, on a particular day. It's a document that, unlike your business plan, looks back rather than forward. Why do you care what your company looks like financially on one particular day of the year? The balance sheet is a useful tool because it helps you assess your projections and where you'd hoped to be. You can measure how far you've come, how close you are to where you want to be, if you exceeded or fell short of want you wanted to accomplish—financially.

The balance sheet shows your assets (accounts receivable, cash, the book value of equipment, property), your liabilities (what you owe), and the difference between the two (your equity). Because it's usually done as of the same day each year, the balance sheet gives you a realistic or reasonable comparison from year to year. Many business owners do an interim financial statement every month, to give them more information, and greater opportunity to react quickly. It doesn't show you how you got there or where you're going; you can't ascertain any trends by studying the balance sheet in isolation. It's only part of the puzzle, but before we look at the other pieces, let's look at the details of the balance sheet and what it *does* tell you.

The balance sheet is divided into three sections: assets, liabilities, and equity. Balance sheets may list these three sections on the right and left (assets on the left, liabilities and equity on the right) or top to bottom (assets on the top, followed by liabilities and finishing with equity). The total assets will always equal the total liabilities and shareholders' (or owners') equity.

> **ASSETS include physical goods and things of value owned by your business.**
>
> *less* **LIABILITIES represent what your business owes (i.e. obligations).**
>
> *equals* **The NET WORTH (owner's equity, shareholder's equity for incorporated companies) is the difference between what your business owns and what it owes.**

People often make their own personal balance sheet—all the things they own, all the things they owe, to give them a personal net worth statement. In your business, the balance sheet tells you what your business owns, what the business owes, and whether the difference is positive or negative. In other words, it shows your net worth, or your equity in the business, on a particular day.

The income statement is also referred to as the profit and loss (P & L) statement or statement of earnings. It shows how much money your business made or lost during a period of time. The income statement matches the revenue generated against all the expenses incurred during the same period. The difference is the net profit or loss for the period.

The statement of financial changes tells you what has changed over that year. Let's look at each of these components in a bit more detail.

The balance sheet should always balance (hence the name!):
Assets = Liabilities + owner's net worth

Net worth   Your equity in your business is determined by the asset and liability equation: Total assets minus total liabilities = your shareholder's equity, or owner's worth. Net worth is also called shareholder's equity or owner's worth, and the different names reflect the different ownership structures. Sole proprietors have net worth or owner's equity because the equity belongs to the sole business owner. Corporations (incorporated companies) have shareholder's equity because companies are owned by shareholders. However, if you own 100% of the shares of your incorporated business, you also own 100% of the shareholder's equity. If you are a 60/40 owner with your spouse, the shareholder's equity is split in the same proportion.

Shareholder's equity is divided into two categories—capital stock and retained earnings. Capital stock represents the owner's equity in the company. Retained earnings are the accumulated total of all the profits—or losses—of the business after taxes are paid. As the business carries on year after year, the profits add to the retained earnings, and the losses subtract from it. The retained earnings are left in the company to help it continue business, to expand, and to invest in new ventures.

Dividends can be paid to the shareholders from the profits of the company. As a 100% owner of the company, you may choose to pay yourself dividends instead of a salary, or a bonus; each has a different tax implication for your personal income tax return.

Income Statement

If the balance sheet is a snapshot, the income statement (also called a profit and loss statement) is more like a video compilation that leads up to the snapshot. In other words, it shows the compressed year-long financial activity that led to the still moment of December 31. It shows the financial effort it took you to get to that one day; it's the financial representation of the blood, sweat, and tears that took you to that one day. It shows the profit or loss made during that year by comparing revenues with expenses undertaken to generate those revenues.

The income statement is set up with net sales at the top, followed by the cost of goods manufactured or sold.

Cost of Goods Sold

In service business cost of goods describes the cost of selling goods.

A manufacturing company includes the cost of the raw materials and the costs of running the factory where the goods are made from those raw materials. Labour and factory overhead are entered separately under cost of goods. From the total of cost of goods is subtracted your unsold inventory; the result is your gross profit.

Operating Expenses

Service businesses as well as manufacturing businesses will have expenses to report. Under the general heading of General and Administrative Expenses, you include such things as the costs of answering the phone, electricity, paper, pencils, costs of gas to get around or travel by public transit, repairs to computer, and so forth. These are all added up and the total appears in this category. A separate category under operating expenses is amortization, following the same principles as outlined earlier.

You also add in, as separate categories, your operating profit (the difference between your gross profit and your operating expenses). Add in other income, subtract other expenses (such as the interest on mortgage payments) to get your net profit before tax. Subtract the tax, and you have your net profit after tax, the final line on the income statement.

Like the balance sheet, an income statement is usually prepared once a year, but when a company is in a period of growth or is struggling to get over a hurdle (such as happened during the ice storm of 1998) the owner may decide that quarterly or even monthly income statements are called for to always be aware of what's actually happening. But if your company has few or no variable costs, an income statement prepared once a year is satisfactory.

You may find that your banker asks for an income statement at a time other than your annual preparation. This could be because the banker has identified a cash crunch in your future or because you're adding a new product or product line or going into a new growth stage. However, if you've kept your finger on the pulse of your business, you probably know long before the banker that you need to make some changes. The more you know what's happening all the time, the more confidence the bank will have in you.

Your Financial Statement

Your accountant may prepare your financial statements in one of three ways:

1. *a compilation*, unaudited financial statements are compiled for a specific purpose; they must be noted as such, since if used for other purposes, they can be misleading. The accountant uses information supplied by the client, but generally accepted accounting principles do not have to be followed and all the information does not have to be accurate; the accountant will preface the report with a "Notice to Reader" that informs the reader that the report contains only limited information that may not have been verified by the accountant. This type of service does not provide the reader any assurance on the reliability of the financial statements.

2. *a review engagement*, in which the auditor reviews the statements to be sure they're plausible mainly by discussion and inquiry with the client; it is not as thorough as an audit but is sufficient for most small business owner's needs—borrowing money or looking for investors. These reports are prepared based on information made available to the accountant and follow generally accepted accounting principles. This type of service provides a higher level of assurance compared to a compilation.

3. *an audited financial statement*, in which the auditor reviews the financial records and operations of the company; the auditor will comb through your files and even talk to suppliers and customers to be sure that invoices have been paid as reported, supplies bought as reported, bank balances are as reported. This type of service provides the highest degree of assurance to the statements' users.

Your Banker and Your Financial Statements

When the bank asks to see financial statements, they will want to see a couple of years' worth, if possible, so they can compare where your business has been and where it is going. The information on one financial statement often covers two years' worth of financial information, so if you can provide two financial statements, you can give your banker a three-year picture (if your business has been operating for that long).

Most business owners only provide financial statements to their banker when they have or are seeking to obtain financing. But providing your financial statements to your banker even before you need money can help you build a relationship that goes far beyond seeking loans. Your banker can make suggestions in areas that you have not had time to focus on or are too close to your business to see. Your banker can also see when you might need some additional financing because your cash flow is getting stretched as your business grows.

A lot of valuable information is hidden within those seemingly dry financial statements. Take the time to learn how they work together and how they work with your business plan.

The charts on the following pages give you a brief overview of the main components of a set of financial statements, what you should know, and how you can use the information for your personal value. A sample set of financial statements is also included to help you through the process.

EXAMPLE: Manufacturing Incorporated Company Balance Sheet

MANFACO INC
Balance Sheet
As at December 31
(in '000 Dollars)

	2001	2000
ASSETS		
Current Assets		
Cash	$ 2	$ 12
Accounts Receivable	80	72
Inventory	153	168
Total Current Assets	235	252
Fixed Assets		
Equipment	64	64
Less Accumulated Amortization	15	30
Net Equipment	49	34
TOTAL ASSETS	284	286
LIABILITIES		
Current Liabilities		
Bank Indebtedness	68	64
Accounts Payable	28	26
Taxes Payable	6	2
Accrued Expenses	5	12
Total Current Liabilities	107	104
Long-Term Liabilities	30	20
TOTAL LIABILITIES	137	124
EQUITY		
Capital Stock	15	15
Retained Earnings	132	147
Total Equity	147	162
TOTAL LIABILITIES AND EQUITY	284	286

EXAMPLE: Manufacturing Incorporated Income Statement

MANFACO INC.
Income Statement
For the years ending December 31
(in 000's of dollars)

	2001	2000
Sales	$ 875	$ 849
Cost of Goods Sold	677	647
Gross Profit	198	202
Operating Expenses		
General Administrative and Selling	152	165
Amortization	15	15
Total Operating Expenses	167	180
Net Operating Profit	31	22
Interest Expense	3	2
Net Profit Before Tax	28	20
Taxes Expense	7	5
Net Income After Tax (Net Income)	21	15

Component of the Balance Sheet of your Financial Statement	What is it?	Why do I care?	What can I do?	What does the banker see and ask about?
ASSETS				
Cash	All the money you have in your bank account and in your till on that business day.	It tells you how much ready cash you had available to pay your bills.	If you have too little, you may need to take steps to collect your receivables or return some inventory to increase the cash you have on hand to pay your employees or pay your rent. If you have too much, it is sitting idle and could be doing better things for you, like making interest in a term deposit or helping you make your business grow.	The amount of cash you have tells your banker if you are prepared to handle your day to day expenses or take advantage of any new business opportunities that might come your way. Is any of the "cash" actually a temporary investment? Can it be cashed in quickly if the business needs it or is it locked in for a longer period of time?
Accounts Receivable	The total of all the money that your customers owe you.	This represents money that is coming into your business for goods or services that customers have already received benefit of, but have not yet paid you for. This is money your business is counting on to be able to pay its bills, its loan payments, its employees.	First, make sure the list is complete. Keep a good record of who owes you money, how much, and for how long. It keeps good relationships with your customers and removes any misunderstandings. Work to collect your accounts receivable in less than 60 days where possible, maximum of 90 days. Unless your customer is of undoubted integrity, the longer it takes for them to pay you, the more you risk not getting your money at all. Don't become a bank for your customers!	The longer your customers take to pay you, the harder it is for you to be able to pay your bills. Your banker will want to know how long money has been owing to you. This is part of "managing your cash flow." You need to know when your money is coming in, when it needs to go out, and that you can count on your customers to pay you when they say they will. Your banker will want to know about your customers—who are they? Where are they? How do they pay you? Is your market growing or declining? Are there new markets for you to expand into?

Component of the Balance Sheet of your Financial Statement	What is it?	Why do I care?	What can I do?	What does the banker see and ask about?
Short-Term Investments	Money that you have invested with a term less than one year. Term deposits and mutual funds are a good example. Shares that you sell on the stock market.	This is money that you have, but may not be able to access quickly if you need it.	When you make your investments, don't just look for the best rate. While it is very important, think about how you might need to use the money and when you might need access. Can you get access to the investment quickly if you need to?	Short-term investments usually tell your banker that you have had some surplus cash available to your business, and that you have some capacity to take on new projects or customers and make your business grow.

They will want to know if you are saving it for an upcoming expense or if it might be securing a loan or letter of credit. If your business is cyclical (busier in some parts of the year than others) it indicates you are aware there are future expenses that may have to be covered from today's efforts. |
| Inventory | The total of all the inventory your business had on hand as of the day of the statement. It is usually valued at cost or current value, whichever is lower.

Inventory could be raw materials, work in progress (partially completed products), or finished goods that your business either made or purchased for resale. | The inventory is what you have available for your customers to purchase. It tells you how much is ready for sale, how much is in progress, and what is sitting as raw materials to be made up into products.

How quickly you turn your inventory into a sale affects how long your cash stays invested in inventory, and how quickly it makes you money. If you can control your inventory closely (don't have any more than you need at any given point) you can free up more cash for operating your business. | Find an effective way to manage your inventory…
• Review it regularly to make sure you aren't keeping too much on hand.
• Look for ways to get rid of the inventory that is obsolete—is there an opportunity to sell it at or close to cost to get your money back?
• If it is raw materials, can you sell them back to the supplier? Or find another business to buy them from you, who may have a better use for them?
• Watch your buying practices. How many people have the authority to make purchases for your company? | How much inventory does your business have that is not making you money, or won't have the chance to make you money in the next 90 days? The next 180 days?

Is there anything you can do to reduce the amount of inventory you have on hand? Is it a reasonable amount for you to do business with?

What kind of arrangements do you have with your suppliers? What happens if you make an error in ordering—will they take it back or are you stuck with it? |

	Keep an eye on whether any of your inventory has become obsolete. Items such as raw materials that you no longer have a use for or finished goods that have been sitting on your shelf for a while are using up valuable cash.	Have they checked to make sure you need to order before they make the order? Nothing worse than getting another shipment of goods before you have even sold the first one out of the last order! • Work to "just in time" delivery from your suppliers. Only keep on hand what you need. Work to establish strong relationships with your suppliers to make sure they will deliver on time, in time, every time. Make sure that if your business grows and you need more inventory you have increased your insurance to cover the higher amount. The same holds true for decreasing your inventory—you can save money on insurance by making sure you have only insured the amount of inventory you carry!	Who does your ordering for inventory, raw materials, or finished products? How are they making sure • there are no double orders, • they are getting the best price, and • they are getting you the best terms for repayment on the inventory? Do you have insurance on your inventory in case of fire or other damage?	
Prepaid Expenses	Your business has paid for something you have not yet received the benefit of. An example—insurance is prepaid for an entire year, but you have only received benefit for 3 months. The remaining 9 months would be a prepaid benefit.	When you review your upcoming expenses for the month, these expenses have already been paid, and you do not have to lay out cash to cover the costs. This is important for your cash flow management.	Some things, like prepaid rent, may only be prepaid for a month. Others, like insurance, might be prepaid for a whole year. To match your revenues and your expenses, consider having the insurance company debit your account each month for 1/12 of the annual bill. If you have too many prepaid expenses, it can really put a damper on your cash flow.	When you have prepaid expenses, it tells your banker that you do not need to set cash aside to pay those expenses in the future. It helps them understand what expenses are upcoming and which ones are already out of the way. If you need short-term financing to cover you until your money comes from your customers, this will be important information for your banker.

Component of the Balance Sheet of your Financial Statement	What is it?	Why do I care?	What can I do?	What does the banker see and ask about?
Property, Plant, and Equipment (Fixed Assets)	Assets that have a value to your business beyond one year, and generally are the assets that help you make money.	These are part of the items your business owns and are usually the ones that generate revenue for the business.	Be prepared to replace your equipment when the time is right. That means when it has outlived its useful life.	Your banker will be looking to understand what your fixed assets do for your business. Is all the equipment relevant to your business operations—that means, will the equipment, machinery, and items listed as fixed assets work for your business to help you generate income? They will want to understand what items don't (things like boats, antique cars, and other items can be found in the financial statement—help the banker understand why they are there).
	They include equipment, machinery, furniture, and other long-lived items that you use to conduct your normal business operations.	Equipment, machinery, computers, furniture often have a life expectancy—that is, a length of time before they wear down or wear out. You will eventually have to replace some or all of the fixed assets your business owns.	Ask yourself if the repairs and maintenance are costing you more than the monthly payment or monthly lease for a new piece that would give you less hassle and less down time.	
	They are stated at cost, less the accumulated amortization, rather than at market or replacement value.	There are times when your fixed assets may actually appreciate in value. Land is an excellent example of this.	Try to maximize the use of each piece of equipment your business owns. If you are a manufacturing company, running an evening shift can give you twice the production from the same piece of equipment. Or maybe you could run two 6-hour shifts instead of one 8-hour shift.	Also, just as you need to understand how you will replace equipment when it wears out or fails, your banker will want to understand that too. Just because you have paid off your equipment doesn't mean it has to be replaced! Again, explain to your banker how you care for it, whether it's insured, or better yet, invite them out to see it!
	Land is the exception. It is always listed at the original cost.		It might be a better idea than adding another piece of equipment, another employee, and more costs.	
Property and Buildings	If you own the land and buildings where your business operates, it is listed here.	The building will depreciate, but the land does not. Land does not "wear out" the way the building and equipment does.	The value of the property and building may grow over time—but it will not change on your balance sheet. You need to recognize the undisclosed value of this asset and ensure your banker does as well!	

Intangible Assets\Goodwill	These are assets that lack physical substance. Examples are copyrights, patents, franchises, trademarks and the goodwill of your business. Intangibles are things you cannot touch or hold, but that add value to your business.	Realize that it can be very difficult to turn these types of assets into cash, unless you are selling your business.	Understand what they are, and what value they give you, and give your business. Goodwill is realized only when your business changes hands.	These are often difficult items to explain, because they aren't tangible —you can't hold them or touch them. Your banker will want to understand their importance, their significance, and their value to your business.
Long-Term Investments	These are investments that your business has made that have a term of longer than one year, or that you do not expect to collect (loans to others) within the next 12 months.	If you decide to make investments in other companies, lend money to employees, or lock your cash up for longer than one year, you should be comfortable that your day-to-day operations of your business will not be negatively affected.	If you end up borrowing at 6% because you locked your money away at 4%, you might wish you hadn't. When you are assessing your cash flow, recognize that this money is not going to be available to you in the next year to help you run the day-to-day operations of your business.	How long is the investment planned for? Is there any access to cash it in in the short term? Your banker may suggest that using the investment, where possible, to secure your loans can save you money on your interest rates. It's an option you should discuss to determine if it is right for you and your business.

LIABILITIES

Bank Debt Notes Payable	This is the balance outstanding on your credit card or operating line as at the date of the balance sheet statement. It may also be money owed to family or friends that you must pay back within the next twelve months.	It tells you how much you owed on your operating line on the date of the statement.	As your business grows, your operating limit may need to change to meet your new day-to-day expenses. If you find you are working within 75% of your limit or more, talk to your banker. You may either need to • find ways to manage your cash to make more of the line available or • increase the line to meet your growing needs.	Your banker will be looking to see if the room you have available on your operating line and in your account can cover your upcoming expenses for your business, including those day-to-day things like rent, utilities, wages, as well as what you owe to your suppliers, your trades, and loan payments that might be coming due.

Component of the Balance Sheet of your Financial Statement	What is it?	Why do I care?	What can I do?	What does the banker see and ask about?
			Also, make sure your operating line isn't carrying the costs of new equipment, computers, or other fixed assets. If you were busy and just wrote a cheque, you may find that it is tying up a large part of your operating line that you need for other things. Talk to your banker about a term loan for your fixed assets.	
Accounts Payable (also called Trade Payables)	The total you owe to your suppliers	This tells you what you owe, and need to have cash to pay for in the near future. The total of your cash in the bank, your available operating line, and the money that is owed to you by your customers should be more than the money you owe on your operating line and you owe in accounts payable.	Managing your trade payables effectively can help you have more money available to meet the day-to-day operating needs of your business.

Take time to work with each of your suppliers—the longer you have a relationship, the more flexible they will be. Can you set terms so that your trades are due in 60 days rather than 30? Or take advantage of discounts that they may offer when you pay cash, or pay within 10 to 30 days?

Don't take for granted that the terms you set up when you opened your business are the ones you should have today. Adding 30 days to the time you have to pay your suppliers can do wonders for your cash flow! | Your banker will want to know how quickly you pay your accounts payable. Is it too soon? Not soon enough? Are you taking advantage of discounts that are available because you have some extra cash?

Can you extend your terms for repayment to give you better access to your cash and better control over your cash flow? |

Current Portion of Long-Term Debt	The amount of money you owe in payments on loans over the next year. This amount represents the current portion (due within the year) of all your loans over 12 months in length. Example: if you have a loan for a piece of equipment and you pay $400 per month for 4 years (48 months) the current portion of your debt would be 12 months x $400 or $4800.	The cash flowing into your business will be used to make these payments. You need to be aware of how much money you have going out, to whom, and when.	Identify which payments are monthly, quarterly, and annual so you can plan to have the money available when you need it. Recognize what interest rates you are paying on your debts, and just like your personal finances, make sure you prepay or pay out the highest interest rate loans first!	Does this include all monthly payments you make? When are they due? Monthly, quarterly, annually?
Long-Term Debts (due sometime longer than one year)	The total amount of money you owe on loans, less the amount that is due within the next year (that is the current portion of your long-term debt above).	These are payments that your business will have to make at some time in the future, a year or more after your statement date.	Determine whether these long-term liabilities are continuations of monthly payments that you are making day to day or whether there are any lump sum payments that you may need to make in the future. Planning ahead can give you peace of mind and let you sleep at night!	Does it reflect all the debts that your company has? Are there any personal debts you carry that are for your business that aren't listed here? Are you taking enough money from the business to make those payments? Or is the business actually paying them?
Contingent Liabilities	Any future obligation you may have, where the exact amount or exact timing of these debts cannot be determined. It could be a guarantee that your company provided to another company, a letter of credit, or letter of guarantee.	This reminds you of potential upcoming costs for you and your business. Try to assess when or if you are likely to have to pay any money out.	If you are aware there is an upcoming expense, you can plan to make sure the money is available when the payment is due. It is no different for contingent liabilities.	How much do you anticipate you will have to pay? Do you have an idea when that might occur? Are you setting any money aside to cover the cost when it comes along?
Net Worth or Owner's Equity (Sole Proprietors and Partnerships) Total Assets Less Total Liabilities = Net Worth or Owner's Worth	The cash that you as the owner (s) have invested into the business to start it, **Plus** Any additional money you may have invested into the business since then **Plus**	This tells you on paper what your business is worth. Remember: it is a snapshot in time, just like a statement you receive from your bank on your investments.	Every time you complete a financial statement you can review your net worth and compare it to your previous statement. If it is getting bigger, you are making a positive impact on your business and personal financial worth. If it is getting smaller, you need to	The net worth tells your banker a few things—whether your business has the ability to grow, and whether you are leaving enough of the profits in the business to be able to manage the day-to-day operations.

Component of the Balance Sheet of your Financial Statement	What is it?	Why do I care?	What can I do?	What does the banker see and ask about?
	Any net profits (after tax) retained in the business.		understand why and what steps you can take to correct it.	It also tells your banker whether you are able to pay yourself, and that's very important. Your banker will want to know that your business is able to provide for the lifestyle that you hope it will.
Shareholder's Equity (Incorporated Companies) Shareholder equity is divided into two categories: Capital Stock—represents the shareholder or owner's equity in the company, and Retained Earnings—the accumulated total of all profits, or losses, of the business, after taxes are paid. Dividends—can be paid to the shareholders from the profits of the company.	The cash that shareholders of an incorporated company invested in the business to start it, **Plus** any additional money they have invested since then, **Plus** any net profit retained in the business.	The shareholder equity tells you the amount of money you have invested as shareholders in the business, and what your business is worth. Again, this is the balance sheet—it is a picture of your business at one point in time. As your business carries on year after year, the profits add to the retained earnings and the losses are subtracted from it. The retained earnings are left in the company to help continue business, to expand, and to invest in new business ventures.	The shareholders' equity helps you establish the value of your business for you and for any other shareholders your business may have. This can be very important to your investors, who may be expecting a return on their investment some day. As with the sole proprietor and partnerships, you will want to compare it to previous balance sheets to determine if the overall worth of your company is increasing or decreasing. Dividends—If you are 100% owner of the company, you may choose to pay yourself dividends instead of a salary, or a bonus—each has a different tax implication for your personal tax return.	Things your banker will look for include: Did you pay any dividends to the shareholders? Does your business have enough equity to be able to grow, or to sustain its current operations?
THE INCOME STATEMENT				
Sales or (Revenue)	The amount of goods or services you sold for cash, or on credit during this reporting period.	This tells you how much your business recorded in sales during the reporting period—it may be for a month, a quarter, a year.	You can use this information to help you understand if your sales are increasing, decreasing, or staying the same. You can see if you have a change or a trend over several months. Sometimes this is the first time you	Are all your sales final sales? Do you have a return policy? How do your sales compare to previous periods? Is your business growing, declining, or staying consistent? What do you want it to do?

		realize just how much your business has grown! When you think back, you will see you are working harder, doing more, with less time for you, and the pace has moved from extremely busy to frantic. Now you can see why—make some decisions for your future! If your sales are declining, you may want to explore new markets, find new customers, or find ways to sell more to your existing customers.	If sales are growing rapidly, your banker will need to know and understand what that means to you. Will you need new employees? Or is it temporary? Are your suppliers ready to work with you as you grow? What will happen to your operating expenses and your cash flow?
Cost of Sales (or Cost of Goods Sold)	The amount that you originally paid to • manufacture your product • purchase the products you sell to your customers • includes freight, duty, shipping, customs costs associated with the goods • includes raw material costs	Businesses that are service related will not have a cost of goods sold. The information or knowledge they sell is different from buying and reselling a product or manufacturing a product.	If you are in a business that has cost of goods sold, you will want to understand the percentage of your cost of goods sold to your sales. If you track this information, you may see that the cost of your goods is going up, and your margins (your gross profit) is going down). Do you need to pass on these increased costs to your customer? Can you? You can also isolate which costs are increasing—perhaps raw materials or products you buy for resale. It might be time to review your options for new suppliers or negotiate new prices with your existing ones.
= Gross Profit (or Loss)	The difference between the revenue and the cost of sales, available for you to pay your expenses, and make your final profit.	Divide your gross profit by your sales. If the percentage is greater than the last time you did this analysis, you are earning more money for each dollar's worth of products you sell. If it is getting lower, you want to get control of	If your goal it to make as much as you can with the least amount of effort, you will want to keep your costs under control. There are two ways to make more money: increase your sales or decrease your expenses. Your banker doesn't want you to work harder either! Talk to her about your costs of sales, how you get your raw materials, and where you get them from.

Component of the Income Statement of your Financial Statement	What is it?	Why do I care?	What can I do?	What does the banker see and ask about?
		your costs as quickly as possible. It means you are working just as hard and making less money doing it.	Better yet, doing both will have an even bigger impact!	Your banker knows lots of other small business owners who may be able to help you out!
+ Other Revenue	May include interest from investments, or rent on property, or other revenue that your business obtains, from sources other than your primary business.	By identifying the sideline business opportunities you have, you can determine whether it is your main business focus that makes you money or the stuff you do on the side.	You may find that those sideline business ventures are costing you more time than they make you, and that you need to keep your focus on your main business. Are you spreading yourself too thin?	
			If you find the other revenue is rewarding your business, keep it up, and think about where your focus should best be.	
			Remember, there is only one of you to go around!	
= Total Gross Profit and Other Revenue	The total of your gross profit and other revenues that your business earned.	This is the amount you have available to cover all your operating expenses for your business. That includes paying yourself.		
EXPENSES				
Selling, General and Administrative Expenses	Amount for salaries, supplies and other costs required to run your business, to generate revenue for your business. Includes rent, utilities, vehicle expenses. Also called Operating Expenses.	Many of these expenses are controllable—every dollar of expense saved is a dollar towards your bottom line.	Review your expenses to look for cost savings and ways to improve your personal wealth by increasing your business profits!	

Interest Expense	Reflects the cost of borrowing money. It might include your operating line, your term loans, your credit card interest, your loans with all finance companies. Some statements break out the short-term interest expense and put it in Administrative expenses; others keep it all together.	The better you can manage when money is paid to you by your customers and when you pay those you owe, the less interest you will pay on your operating line or credit card! Also, keep your eyes out for those term loans that have high interest rates. If you have spare cash and want to prepay or payout a debt, get rid of the highest-cost ones first.	Work on keeping your accounts receivable current! In other words, know who owes you money, and when it is due, and work with your customer to collect as early as possible. Keep your inventory as low as possible to keep your business running effectively, and keep your customers satisfied. Look for just-in-time delivery so you don't end up using your operating line to pay for goods that may sit for months on your shelf before they make you money! Work to keep your accounts payable in check. Make arrangements with your suppliers to pay in 60 or 90 days, whenever possible...seek discounts when you pay early!
Amortization	A way to calculate and write off the costs of fixed assets (machinery buildings, equipment, etc.) which wear out over time or become obsolete over time. The equipment, machinery, and other fixed assets you buy have a limited useful life, after which time they become worn out or obsolete. The amortiztion process sets an expiration date for the life of the fixed asset, and distributes the value over its estimated useful life. It is a process of allocation of expense, not a valuation of the equipment.	The cost of your equipment or machinery wearing out due to use is an expense to your business. Every time you use the equipment to help you generate revenue, you are wearing it out or wearing it down. Over time, the equipment becomes worth less than when you purchased it. You need to be able to expense the cost of using your equipment to do business in the same time frame that you use the equipment to generate revenues.	Remember, this is a non-cash transaction...you don't need to pay out any money today. But you will have to plan to replace the fixed asset, the equipment, or the machinery sometime. Amortization is an expense or a cost of doing business. Every year, you can deduct the allocated amortization amount from your income, reducing the overall profits and the amount you are required to pay tax on. The amount expensed to your business as amortization is a non-cash transaction—you didn't actually have to spend the money to pay for amortization. Your banker will want to know your amortization expense, because it can be added back into your cash available to service your loan payments, or grow your business, or manage your day-to-day expenses.

Component of the Income Statement of your Financial Statement	What is it?	Why do I care?	What can I do?	What does the banker see and ask about?
= Net Income (Loss) Before Taxes	Tells you the profitability of your business after your expenses, but before you pay taxes on the income.	This is the excess you have after your cost of goods, and your operating expenses.	Remember, this number is only as good as the records you keep! If you have misplaced your receipts or haven't got everything recorded, you may be fooling yourself into thinking you are making money when you aren't. On the other hand, if you haven't accounted for all the sales, you could be "selling yourself short."	Your banker will be interested in comparing this information with previous statements, whether they are monthly, quarterly, or annual. Most of all, your banker is looking to see if you are on track to achieve your business and personal financial goals, and offering some suggestions to help you get there. As with all the information on the financial statement, it can help to compare it to previous records. That will help your banker determine what financial solutions they might suggest—everything from your financing needs, to investments, to accessing your banking on-line.
- Income Tax Expense	This is the amount you must pay to the government for income tax on your business.	When you see this amount on your statement, it doesn't necessarily mean that it is paid, but that it must be paid. Depending on your business, you have probably been paying instalments monthly or quarterly already, and if you aren't you might want to think about doing it. It can be a lot less painful than paying once a year.	One of the benefits of having an accountant, bookkeeper, CA, CMA, or CGA working on your team is that they will make every effort to keep what you pay in income tax as low as possible.	It is important to pay your income tax on time, if only for the fact that late payments have late fees assessed, and the interest charges cost your business money. There are many ways you can save your business money, and paying on time, in this case, is one of them! Your bank can offer to set you up for on-line banking, so you can pay your source deductions and government remittances right on-line! Saves you time and money.
= Net Income (Loss) After Taxes	Shows you the effect of taxes on your profitability.	It's part of the cost of success! If your business does well, you should expect	Think about how you will use this money for your business in the future.	

to pay taxes. And once you get over the fact that you have to give some of your hard-earned money to the government, recognize that having to pay taxes can be a good problem to have...

+ Extraordinary Gains	These are things that are not part of normal operations of your business. They might be a result of discontinuing part of your operations and selling the equipment, or sale of a building or property.	This highlights extraordinary or unusual events that your business has had in the past, and that you do not expect to happen again.	Your banker will want to know that these extraordinary items were. If they involved selling a piece of equipment you have to replace, you might be needing a new term loan!
- Extraordinary Losses	Sometimes when you sell the equipment or the building, you sell it for less than you paid for it, or less than you accounted for in your financial statements.	Extraordinary losses may have a positive impact on the amount of tax you have to pay!	
= Net Income (Loss) After Taxes and Extraordinary Items	The cumulative effect of all gains and losses included on the income statement for this reporting period.	This is the net amount that your business made after all expenses, all taxes, all unusual activities. It is the amount that your net worth or shareholder's equity will increase or decrease by in this reporting period.	If your business made money (at least on paper) you should take some time to reflect on your success and give yourself a pat on the back for all your hard work. If it didn't (at least on paper) make sure you take some time with your trusted advisors to talk about what worked and what you can change to make your business more successful. Sometimes nothing needs to change, you just need to be patient. The revenues and the profits are just over the horizon. And don't lose sight of why you got into business in the first place.

This is where you will want to continue to share with your banker your longer term goals for your business. If you are adapting or changing your business to achieve new or modified goals, keep your banker current. And that goes for your personal life as well. An addition to the family, marriage, divorce, and death can all affect your personal and financial goals.

It is important to keep your banker focused on what it is you are trying to accomplish, so they can review your financial information with that in mind.

Get the most from your banker!

Ten Top Tax Tips

We've all heard about that famous bottom line—the phrase has moved into the realm of cliché and is now applied to matters beyond the business world. But for most small business owners, that's what the financial statements come down to: the bottom line. Am I making enough when all the financial information is categorized, added, and subtracted? If you're not happy with your bottom line, there might be some easy ways to improve it. Reducing your taxes is a great way to improve the bottom line and one that often gets overlooked. We all have a vested interest in paying taxes, and I'm not suggesting you avoid doing so. But we all also want to be careful and responsible with our money, and good tax planning is a time-honoured way of doing that. Look to the professionals to give you advice on this. Your banker can make suggestions, but your banker is not a trained tax professional. You need your accountant or a tax lawyer to steer you straight.

Consider the following ways to minimize your tax bill:

1. Interest you pay on money you borrow to run your business is deductible. The link between the borrowed money and the use must be clear and direct in order to be eligible. Example: If you've been saving for a new computer and were planning on putting your Mexican vacation on credit, think again. Use the cash for your holiday (and you probably won't spend as much!) and borrow to buy the computer.

2. A corporation is a separate legal entity, so the losses it incurs can't be claimed by its shareholders. Loans advanced to a corporation by a shareholder may be deductible as an allowable business investment loss (ABIL). Example: Let's say your incorporated business is in need of $20,000 cash to purchase a new piece of equipment and it does not have the funds available. You, as a shareholder, do. If you "lend" the money to the business, it is called a shareholder loan. If the business loses money, you may be able to claim a portion of the loss (related to your loan) on your personal income tax. Your accountant will help you with this.

3. Hire your spouse and children to work for you. You must pay them a reasonable salary, but it becomes a business expense deductible for income tax purposes.

4. If you are paying tax by quarterly instalments, always pay on time or you will be charged interest and potentially a late penalty; you have better things to do with your money than pay it out this way.

5. If you owe money to Canada Customs and Revenue Agency (formerly Revenue Canada) and can't pay the full amount immediately, negotiate an acceptable payment arrangement with them so that they don't seize any of your assets.

6. If you are the owner of an incorporated company and pay yourself a salary, you are not eligible for Employment Insurance as an owner-manager, so you should not make any remittance when you complete your personal income tax return.

7. Reasonable expenses for meals and entertainment incurred for the purpose of earning business income are deductible at 50% of the total for income tax purposes.

8. Self-employed people who work out of their home can deduct moving expenses if they move to a new home more than 40 kilometres away, the same way employees can when they move to a new job or take an employment transfer.

9. Self-employed people may be allowed to deduct on their income tax return the costs of attending up to two conventions a year in connection with their business or profession.

10. If you own your own business and are retiring to leave it for others to carry on, you can arrange for the company to pay you a reasonable retiring allowance, which will be deductible to the company, and you may be able to transfer all or a portion of the allowance to your RRSP and claim the tax deduction.

11 Selling Your Business

Planning how you will sell your business or when you will close it should start almost the day you go into business. It's not surprising that it's just about the last thing on people's minds at that time. It's true, you were looking to the future when you were getting your new business up and running but, you'd probably say, not *that* far forward! It makes sense to start early. You want to be in a position to sell a healthy, thriving business so you can start another business or retire. That means monitoring the health of your company by reviewing your business plan regularly, tracking your cash flow, and studying and analyzing your financial statements. If the sale of your business is the foundation for your retirement years, are you on target to realize that amount when it comes time to sell? Is selling even an option for you? If you're going to start another business, will the sale of this business yield enough money to start your new business?

Every few months ask yourself, "Am I building something worth buying?" It's a reminder that your business is your investment in your future.

Thinking Ahead

Selling. Your business will be valuable to a prospective buyer only if it is profitable. If you were buying a business today, would you buy yours? Consider the amount of time, energy, and money you put into it. Given the profit and lifestyle it affords you, what's it worth? Could you expect someone else would want to buy your business on the same terms? As you revisit your business plan on a regular basis, make this question part of that exercise: What can I be doing to make my business attractive when it's time to sell?

Retiring. If you've been planning your retirement strategy from the day you started your business, chances are you'll have been contributing to your RRSPs, paying off your mortgage, setting a little aside regularly to make some investments so you'll have a retirement income you can count on and to minimize the tax you pay now.

If you have been relying 100% on you business to provide you with your retirement wealth, you need to give yourself some peace of mind, and make sure that retirement will be everything you need and want it to be.

Some businesses do not have fixed assets such as machinery or equipment that can be sold to fund your retirement. In this situation, you'll need to know where your income will come from when you retire. In the service area, businesses rarely have significant fixed assets, so RRSPs and long-term investment planning might be right for you. The same principles apply as for long-term investing for any purpose: invest a little at a time, all the time, for the long term, and diversify your investments.

RRSPs are not the solution for everyone. Farmers, for example, may see their land as their retirement fund by renting it out or selling it. Should he decide to sell, the farmer will have the proceeds from the sale of the land to fund his retirement; renting gives him a steady income. Putting money into an RRSP for deferred income-tax planning may not have given that farmer the benefits he was looking for. The important thing is to choose the method that's best for you and review it every year to be sure it's still the best option. There are oodles of financial planners, investment specialists, and brokers available to provide you excellent investment advice. Again, find one who understands the small business owner.

Selling a Business

What brings owners to the stage of wanting to sell the business they've nurtured? Just as with starting a business, there are as many reasons as there are individuals, but we can find some common threads:

- A new business opportunity appears.
- A better business opportunity appears!
- The business is growing beyond the ability of the owner and there is an opportunity to make money by selling it.

- It's time to retire.
- The owner is ill or has been injured.
- A member of the family is ready to take over the business, leaving the owner to retire or start a new business.
- Partnership disputes have led to such acrimony that the partnership has to be dissolved and the business sold or one partner buys the other out. In partnerships, the illness or death of one partner can cause the other to sell the business.
- Sometimes a business owner just loses interest; perhaps something else has come along that's more appealing or the owner found being the sole proprietor of a small business different than expected.
- Reasons for selling a business may be connected to not having enough working capital to grow the business; perhaps the owner doesn't have the skill or desire to take it to the next level.
- The business is losing money. This is always a sad situation, for dreams are shattered. If the business is faltering, it will be difficult to sell it.

Selling a business is like selling a house in that you should do the equivalent of leaving simmering cinnamon-spiced apple cider on the stove when prospective purchasers come calling: make sure the premises are clean and tidy, all equipment is in good working order, and the inventory is current. That said, selling a business is really not like selling a house—it could take a year or more to find the right buyer, and during that time you have to keep the business as prosperous as possible so that it's attractive to potential buyers. If you have employees, you need to keep them motivated and interested in staying with your company once word is out that you're selling. Don't forget your creditors and customers—once they know you're selling, they too will need assurance that the business is healthy and will continue to operate.

It's hard sometimes to keep your selling preparations quiet, but it's important to make the attempt. As I suggested above, employees and customers may take fright and start looking around for other employers and suppliers. Before you're ready to let people know your plans, you may be asked straight out, "Are you selling?" Practise responding to this question so you're not caught off guard. You may not want to admit that you are thinking of selling, but there are ways of dealing with this question without actually lying (never never do that!). "Buyers have approached me over the years, and that usually leads to rumours" or "Everything's for sale at a price" are two time-tested responses. A bit of humour never hurts: "Did you bring your chequebook?" or "Show me the money!" can deflect the most persistent questioners.

When you've reached that point of actively preparing to sell, put together a package that you can give to prospective buyers. Consider designing it so that it doesn't have to be released all at once. You may talk to many people who are not really interested in your business to buy, but as a source of information. These people might be your potential competitors, and if you reveal to them the inner workings of the company before you know they are serious and in a position to buy, you could be giving away valuable information. Remember that your business is now the product you're selling. Your package should contain the following topics, although not all of them should be made available to everyone:

- A history of your business and why you're selling
- A description of how the business operates
- Information about the facilities
- Information about your suppliers
- A profile of the market, your customer base, and the competition
- An organizational chart if you have staff; include rates of pay and indicate those who've shown a willingness to stay on after a sale
- Review of your insurance coverage
- Outline of any outstanding legal matters
- Three to five years of accurate financial statements
- Itemized tangible and intangible assets so the prospective buyer will know what they can borrow against should they need to
- The price, which you should justify by referring to expected investment returns; this will enable interested parties to estimate how long it will take to get their initial investment back
- Customer testimonials to demonstrate their loyalty to the company
- A confidentiality agreement, which will benefit both buyer and seller

As you talk with prospective buyers, remember:
Desire to buy is not proof of ability to buy. Make sure your potential buyer is sincere before your release all your information.

As you gather together these documents, think about what your business means to you. This may be an emotional time for you, for so much of who you are is tied to your business. After all, you created it! What value does the goodwill of your business have to a potential buyer? The lifestyle your business gives you and the revenue it generates are both important factors in the value of your business; so are the fixed and movable assets and the inventory. Setting the price on your business doesn't have to be tricky, especially if you work with a broker.

Your Sales Team

Just as you've done throughout the life of your business, you'll be working with your team—lawyer, banker, and accountant. You may consider adding someone else for this one important step. Selling your business can be a daunting prospect, so look into working with a broker or a Certified Business Valuator (CBV) who specializes in these matters, especially if you can find one who specializes in selling small businesses. Your lawyer, banker, and accountant will likely be able to recommend someone to you. All of these people will want to be part of the new team working with the new owner, so they have a vested interest in making the experience as positive as possible for you, the broker, and the new owner.

> **The Web site for the Canadian Institute of Chartered Business Valuators is www.cicbv.ca.**

Brokers usually work for an accounting firm—it's one of the services offered by most of the larger firms. You'll pay a percentage of the sales price to the broker, but by now you'll know whether this is something you'd rather hand off to someone else or something you'd like to tackle.

Interview several brokers to assess what each knows about the kind of business you're in and to see which you feel comfortable with. Does the broker or CBV seem honest with you; for example, if he thinks you're asking too much for the business, how does he deal with that discussion? Don't choose someone just because she quotes you the highest price for your business, either. Unrealistic expectations can lead to hard feelings all round and affect the price you actually get when you make your deal. Some people will quote a price that seems high because they think that's what you want to hear. In the end, however, to sell your business, you may have to drop the price and end up taking less than you would have realized if you'd set a more realistic price.

The services offered by a CBV include any or all of the following:

- Price the business
- Set the terms of sale
- Put together the package
- Market your business
- Identify potential buyers
- Screen interested buyers
- Negotiate and evaluate the offers
- Oversee the legal process

If you decide to sell the business yourself, keep the above list in mind, contracting out the parts you don't feel qualified to do or don't have the time to do. To get the word out that you're selling, talk to suppliers and customers, again reassuring them that you're still in business and are highly motivated to keep the business running well in the coming months. Run ads in the classified section of your local paper. Don't identify your company but give a brief description of your business. Provide a phone number or box number so that interested parties can reach you. If you belong to a trade or professional association that publishes a journal, you might decide to advertise in that publication.

With your team, discuss who might be interested in buying your business. They can help you decide issues such as how much cash the purchaser needs. If you have a broker on your team, let her weed out the tire-kickers— you've still got a business to run. When it comes time to interview the interested parties, if you're doing it yourself, remember that your goal is to sell the business, not to beat the other party into submission. Keep your passion for your business and your emotions concerning selling it in check. You've probably had some practice at this already over your business life, but selling the business, whether for happy or not-so-happy reasons, can be even more emotional than starting the business. If a broker or CBV is involved, they have to stay neutral, avoiding disputes, but resolving them if they arise.

Setting the Price

Setting the price is one of the most difficult parts of selling a business, as it is with a house, and the results can be just the same. If you set the price too high, you may end up with less than if you'd set the price a bit lower but more realistic.

As you might gather from that equation, an appraiser, or Certified Business Valuator, can make your job easier, and setting the price is definitely one aspect you might be glad to hand over. It removes that emotional side of the process, for the appraiser will apply one of three basic methods for evaluating your business.

The first is "capitalization of earnings." Under this method, the appraiser will calculate the profitability of the company and assess a value for the profits that will be generated in the future. The assumption is that the company will continue to produce profits every year for a certain number of years—three to five years is the usual time span. Profits from the previous and current years are averaged, and the average is multiplied by a factor that is contingent on the industry and the management.

The second method is "book value." For this, the evaluator goes to the balance sheet, takes the total assets, subtracts the liabilities, and the result is the book value. For example, if your total assets in your most recent balance sheet were $900,000 and your total liabilities were $400,000, the book value would be the difference between the two: $500,000.

The third method, "economic appraisal," is not as cut-and-dried as the previous two methods. It includes placing a value on such intangibles as customer loyalty and management capacity and can vary in the way it is approached. Intuition plays a role and is best left to the experts. Of course, the basics of the first two methods are part of this economic appraisal, too: the company's profit history, the condition of the company (this refers to everything from the state of the equipment to the state of the books), prevailing economic conditions, and the expectation for profits in the future. Each method is likely to come up with a different value and each should be considered on its own merits when establishing the final asking price for your business.

> **The buyer is buying for the future, not the past. Projected earnings, therefore, are more important to the buyer than past earnings, and will most likely be considered when valuing your business.**

When you finally come up with a price you're all comfortable with, in the final negotiations, be prepared to take less. Like selling a house, negotiation is going to be part of the sale.

Making the Deal

When it comes time for a buyer to make an offer, you will need to release various financial documents. This is the point at which the confidentiality agreement should be considered.

If your business is a sole proprietorship or partnership, you and the buyer will be involved in what's known as an asset transaction. The assets being bought will be detailed in the contract. Usually, the buyer buys everything the company owns except cash, accounts receivable, and liabilities. You will be expected to pay off all short- and long-term liabilities from the proceeds you receive. Discuss the tax implications of this type of transaction with your accountant.

If your business is a corporation, you will most likely sell your shares to the new owner. All aspects of the business continue; the assets and the liabilities of the business carry on as if nothing has happened.

If the new owner already has a company, or wants to establish a new incorporated business, your business can sell its assets to the new business. You will remain the shareholder to the original company, and the proceeds from the sale are paid to the business, not to you. There are very different tax implications in each of these scenarios, and you should discuss them at length with your accountant or lawyer.

At some point an offer will be made to you, so run through the various scenarios you might find yourself in. The broker, who will have amassed useful advice from being involved in many sales, can give you an idea of what's to come. Get the tough issues out of the way first and remember to think of the buyer as your ally. You're working with her to come up with solutions, options, and alternatives during the negotiating process. Be prepared to consider some of the following:

- *The buyer pays you cash, outright.* The buyer may have put a loan in place, or used some personal assets to invest, but you don't care; the fact of the matter is you have a clean sale, money passes hands, and you walk away. This is the best type of sale you can hope for. Make sure your accountant or financial adviser helps you manage the tax implications!

- *The buyer will ask to pay you over time.* This is not unusual; in fact, an all-cash deal may not be in the cards. Expect to receive a down payment, but the new owner may want to pay the remaining amount through a promissory note, using the assets of the business as security, that is paid off over a specified period of time with a specified interest rate (this interest rate could also be tied to the prime rate in some way, and thus may vary over the life of the note). Your future and your ability to manage your new business, your retirement, your personal debts can be affected by this type of transaction. Make sure your lawyer, accountant, and banker have done their due diligence—detailed checking—to help you determine if this is a reasonable solution for you. If you need all your money now, it may not be.
- *The buyer will propose a leveraged buyout.* This method is also secured by the assets of the business, but the buyer invests little or none of his own money, borrowing from a bank or other similar institution. Leveraged buyouts place a heavy debt burden on the company, and you and the new owner must be confident that the business will be able to service the debt.

With each of these methods, and any other payment methods that are presented to you, think about how they will affect your retirement or the new business you're entering.

Remember that you should be working together with the buyer to come to the deal that is best for both of you. Negotiations over matters such as the above can go back and forth as you work out the details. Your strength is that you know your company and its place in your industry, so you will be able to defend both the price and the terms you seek.

You and the buyer should understand why you're selling and she's buying, what motivates both of you, why you've taken a certain stand on an issue. Be prepared to defend your positions with facts and try to anticipate arguments and positions coming from the buyer so that you can be ready to respond to them. Many prospective owners can be inquiring about your business at the same time, just as when you sell your house. However, once you start the bidding process, it is ethical to deal with only one offer at a time.

The Offer
The offer should contain the following items:

- The price being offered
- How much is being offered as a security deposit and down payment, and how much is being financed
- Assets and liabilities being purchased
- Operating condition of equipment at the time the sale closes
- A stipulation that the business will be able to pass any necessary inspection
- The right to subtract from the purchase price any undisclosed liabilities that come due after settlement
- Warranties of clear title, and the validity of existing contracts, including an assurance that they can be transferred to the buyer
- A provision that the sale is contingent on such things as lease assignment, verification of financial statements, transfer of licences, obtaining of financing, and so on
- A provision for expenses that have been paid—rent, utilities, wages, and so forth
- An undertaking called a non-competition covenant. This prohibits you from going into business as a direct competitor with the new owner.
- Outline of how the company is to be operated until settlement
- Date of settlement

Take the time to go over the offer carefully. You can ask for a financial statement from the buyer and even a post-sale business plan. Involve your accountant and lawyer in the review of the offer and be prepared for some back-and-forthing as the details are worked out. Be sure there is a nonrefundable deposit—deals do fall apart!

In Closing
When you and the buyer have worked out the details and have a signed agreement, your lawyer will take you through the steps to bring the transaction to a close. Be sure you know at each step what is happening, what you are signing, and when you have to meet certain conditions. Once the buyer's cheque has cleared and the funds are in your account, your business is sold and you can get on with the rest of your life.

As you work through these stages, you will slowly be saying goodbye to your company and the people you've met through the years. But you'll also be saying hello to the next stage of your life—retirement, a new business, or the pursuit of another interest such as finishing off a university degree or sailing around the world! If you're like the small business owners I've met over the years, I know you'll be doing something active and interesting. The characteristics that made you a successful small business owner and the experience you gained will continue to serve you well.

Appendix: Resources for Small Business Owners

Throughout the life of your business, you'll amass a great many helpful phone and fax numbers, addresses, Web sites, e-mail addresses, and names. Here are some to help you get started and to add to your own list.

General Information

Better Business Bureau
www.canadiancouncilbbb.ca
44 Byward Market Square
Suite 220
Ottawa, Ontario
K1N 7A2
(613) 789-5151
Fax (613) 789-7044
Contact the national office to find your nearest office. They will tell you whether there have been any complaints lodged against any customer or supplier you're thinking of doing business with.

BusinessGateway.ca
http://businessgateway.ca
This Web site is a good place to start for general business information, services, and resources that are available to support Canadian business.

Canada Business Service Centres
www.cbsc.org
This collaboration between federal, provincial, and private-sector organizations is a must-visit for small business owners. Start with the Web site, which can direct you to your local office if need be. You'll find information on government services, programs, and regulations affecting businesses. This one-stop site tells you how to start a business in Canada, covering topics such as market assessment, financing, taxation, and writing a business plan. Check out the sub-site Business Start-Up Assistant at **http://bsa.cbsc.org**. You can also find out about registering your business at **www.cbsc.org/osbw/busforms.html** and click on your province. A business plan can be found at **www.cbsc.org/ibp** and **www.cbsc.org/osbw/sample.html**.

CanadaOne
www.canadaone.com
This free on-line Canadian business magazine is aimed directly at small business owners. The site has information about the best structure for your company; answers to questions concerning everything from borrowing, to being an employer, to applying for grants; lists of upcoming events, such as seminars and workshops that are of interest to small business owners; and a wide variety of technical tips sent in by visitors to the site.

Canadian Association of Family Enterprise
www.cafeuc.org/about/chapters.html
25750 Dunwin Drive
Mississauga, Ontario
L5L 3N9
(905) 569-7248
This organization for family-run companies has chapters across Canada; the Web site takes you to a list of their local chapters where you can get addresses and phone numbers. CAFE provides educational programs, mentoring, and peer advisory groups for family-run companies.

Canadian Chamber of Commerce
www.chamber.ca
Delta Office Tower
350 Sparks Street
Suite 501
Ottawa, Ontario
K1R 7S8
(613) 238-4000, (416) 868-6415
Fax (613) 238-7643
Check with your local chamber of commerce for relevant workshops or seminars; they can also provide help with networking.

Canadian Federation of Independent Business
www.cfib.ca
(416) 222-8022
A worthwhile site to visit—with links to other sites, such as one at Strategis (see below) that helps you calculate whether it's better to lease or buy. It also offers members the opportunity to apply for merchant credit card status at preferred rates with selected banks. You can check the federation's national or provincial activities.

Entrepreneurship Institute of Canada
www.entinst.ca
P.O. Box 40043
75 King Street South
Waterloo, Ontario
N2J 4V1
1-800-665-4497
Fax (519) 885-0990
Order books, videos, software and CDs of interest to small business owners.

Human Resources Development Canada
www.hrdc-drhc.gc.ca
With offices across Canada, HRDC offers information on programs and services for small business in Canada; also advises on counselling and training new employees; and provides initiatives to unemployed people who want to start a business. They also have information about the Student Business Loan Program.

ProfitGuide
www.profitguide.com
Much more than an on-line version of *PROFIT*, a magazine for Canadian entrepreneurs, this Web site is a business resource for Canadian entrepreneurs. Scotiabank is one of its sponsors.

Retail Council of Canada
www.retailcouncil.org
121 Bloor Street East
Suite 1210
Toronto, Ontario
M4W 3M5
1-888-373-8245, (416) 922-6678
Fax (416) 922-8011
The large Web site contains information of interest to retailers, many of whom are small business owners; on-line retailers are also represented.

Strategis
http://strategis.ic.gc.ca
A large Web site managed by Industry Canada, it has a special section for small businesses, including information on the Canada Small Business Financing program. The Canadian Bankers Association says it's Canada's largest business information Web site and has useful advice about other resources and organizations.

Credit Bureaus

These organizations will give you information about your credit report so you can be sure it's correct and up to date.
Dun & Bradstreet Canada
www.dnb.ca
577 Hurontario Street
Mississauga, Ontario
L5R 3G5
(905) 568-6000
Fax (905) 568-6197

Equifax Canada Inc.
www.equifax.ca
Box 190 Jean Talon Station
Montreal, Quebec
H1S 2Z2
1-800-465-7166 or (514) 493-2314

Trans Union of Canada
www.tuc.ca
Consumer Relations Department
P.O. Box 338-LCD1
Hamilton, Ontario
L8L 7W2
(905) 575-4420

Education

Canada Customs and Revenue Agency—Small Business Information Seminar
www.ccra-adrc.gc.ca/tax/business/smallbusiness/sbis-e.html
CCRA offers a free small business information seminar program aimed primarily at the small business entrepreneur. If you're about to start a business or have just begun to operate a business, check this one out.

CBSC Online Small Business Workshops
www.cbsc.org/osbw
An on-line workshop for small business owners about the various issues in starting and operating a business.

CMA-Canada
www.cma-canada.org
Click on "Courses and Conferences" to learn about their on-line courses that help small business owners gain knowledge in managing the affairs of their business, including financial statements, Internet knowledge, and e-commerce.

Government of Canada—Small Business Info-Fairs
http://strategis.ic.gc.ca/sc_mangb/fairs/engdoc/homepage.html
A showcase of federal government programs and services and "how-to" seminars for small business.

VUSME

www.vusme.org

VUSME makes on-line learning modules available through organizations that support and service the small business community. The courses help small business owners gain knowledge in managing the affairs of their business, including financial statements, Internet knowledge, and e-commerce. Free trial courses available. Scotiabank has partnership with them.

Exporting

Canadian Commercial Corporation

www.ccc.ca

1100–50 O'Connor Street

Ottawa, Ontario

K1A 0S6

1-800-748-8191, (613) 996-0034

Fax (613) 995-2121

The corporation provides access to overseas market opportunities and export contracting services.

Department of Foreign Affairs and International Trade

www.dfait-maeci.gc.ca

1-800-267-8376

The place to start to look for information about opportunities and requirements for exporting abroad.

Export Development Corporation

www.edc-see.ca

151 O'Connor Street

Ottawa, Ontario

K1A 1K3

1-800-850-9629, (613) 598-2500

Fax (613) 237-2690

Offers financing help for small businesses, insurance information, and other finance services for exporters and investors.

ExportSource
http://exportsource.gc.ca
ExportSource is an on-line resource for export information. It provides a single access point to all trade-related government departments and agencies.

Financial

Business Development Bank of Canada
www.bdc.ca
1-888-INFO BDC
Self-described as Canada's small business bank, the BDC offers financial and consulting services to small and medium-sized businesses. It has more than 80 branches throughout Canada.

Canadian Bankers Association
www.cba.ca
You'll find a small business section with links to all banks and their small business products.

Canadian Institute of Chartered Business Valuators
www.cicbv.ca
277 Wellington Street West
Toronto, Ontario
M5V 3H2
(416) 204-3396
Fax (416) 977-8585
Whether you're buying or selling, start here to find out about valuing the business.

Canadian Institute of Chartered Accountants
www.cica.ca
277 Wellington Street West
Toronto, Ontario
M5V 3H2
1-800-268-3793
(416) 977-3222
Fax (416) 977-8585
Find a chartered accountant or learn more about chartered accountancy by visiting the Web site.

Canadian Venture Capital Association
www.cvca.ca
234 Eglinton Avenue East
Suite 301
Toronto, Ontario
M4P 1K5
(416) 487-0519
Fax (416) 487-5899

The organization's mission statement states that it was founded "to promote the use of venture capital to support the development of small and medium-sized growth businesses in Canada" and to provide a forum for people engaged in venture capital investment in Canada.

Certified General Accountants Association of Canada
www.cga-canada.org

CGA-Canada's SME Centre provides research on questions relevant to small and medium-sized businesses. The site has links to provincial pages.

Farm Credit Corporation
www.fcc-sca.ca
1800 Hamilton Street
P.O. Box 4320
Regina, Saskatchewan
S4P 4L3
1-800-387-3232, (306) 780-8100
Fax (306) 780-5495

This government organization provides financial services to farms and agribusinesses. Includes products, services, publications, and career opportunities.

ROYNAT Capital
www.roynat.com
40 King Street West
Scotia Plaza, 26th Floor
Toronto, Ontario
M5H 1H1
(416) 933-2730
Fax (416) 933-2783
ROYNAT Capital provides financing for the small and medium business market. They consider not only asset-based decisions but also the quality of management, historical performance of the company, cash flow, and broader industry trends when they make their decisions. Long-term capital is their specialty for growing businesses.

Franchises

Canadian Franchise Association
www.cfa.ca
2585 Skymark Avenue
Suite 300
Mississauga, Ontario
L4W 4L5
1-800-665-4232, (905) 625-2896
Start at this Web site to learn about franchising, find franchising opportunities, even learn about job openings.

Human Resources

Human Resources Management
www.hrmanagement.ca
This site, managed by Human Resources and Development Canada, provides small- and medium-sized employers with information on hiring, training and development, labour laws, local business resources, forms and tools.

Internet Business

Ebiz.Enable

http://strategis.ic.gc.ca/sc_indps/ebiz/engdoc/homepage.php

Industry Canada's e-business portal for small- and medium-sized businesses. This is an excellent Web site for small businesses to find e-business related issues.

Electronic Commerce in Canada

http://e-com.ic.gc.ca

This federal government Web site contains useful information on electronic commerce, including articles, tools, statistics, and research reports.

Microsoft bCentral

www.bcentral.com

Get on the Internet with this software, which is designed for small businesses. It includes components for e-commerce, e-mail marketing, finance, appointment scheduling, and more.

Regional

Atlantic Canada Opportunities Agency

www.acoa.ca

Blue Cross Centre, 3rd Floor

644 Main Street

P.O. Box 6051

Moncton, New Brunswick

E1C 9J8

1-800-561-7862, (506) 851-2271

Fax (506) 851-7403

People in the Atlantic region who are setting up new businesses or expanding existing ones can receive information about financing, preparing business plans, and much more from this federal agency.

Canada Economic Development for Quebec Regions
www.dec-ced.gc.ca
1-800-322-4636, (514) 496-4636
The goal of this federal program is to promote economic development in the regions of Quebec where growth is slow. They are particularly interested in working with small- and medium-sized businesses in a wide variety of initiatives.

Federal Economic Development Initiative for Northern Ontario
http://fednor.ic.gc.ca
1-800-461-6021, (705) 942-1327
A program of Industry Canada, FedNor advises businesses in northern Ontario about getting started, selling in the international market, and selling to government, among other initiatives.

Government of Canada
www.businessregistration.gc.ca
If you live in Nova Scotia, you can register your business on-line at this Web site.

Ontario Business Connects
www.cbs.gov.on.ca/obc/english/4TJTBS.htm
Register your business in Ontario through this Web site.

Western Economic Diversification Canada
www.wd.gc.ca
1-888-338-9378
This federally sponsored program offers a range of services for small- and medium-sized businesses in western Canada.

Research

Canadian Company Capabilities
http://strategis.ic.gc.ca/sc_coinf/ccc/engdoc/homepage.html

Canadian Trade Index
www.ctidirectory.com/index.htm

Canada 411: Find a Business
http://canada411.sympatico.ca/eng/business.html
You'll find information about different companies at these sites.

Canadian Business Map
http://strategis.ic.gc.ca/scdt/businessmap/engdoc/0.html
Look for Canadian business information at this site.

GDSourcing
www.gdsourcing.com
Start your market research at this Web site, a directory of Statistics Canada data and other Canadian statistics.

Statistics Canada
www.statcan.ca
The official source for Canadian social and economic statistics.

Taxes

Canada Customs and Revenue Agency
www.ccra-adrc.gc.ca
Formerly Revenue Canada, CCRA offers information booklets, seminars, and other related information of interest to small business owners. Do a search on their site for small business and you'll be presented with an array of choices, including information on the GST/HST.

For information about registering for the GST/HST, go to **www.ccra-adrc.gc.ca/tax/business/gsthst/menu-e.html**. To find out about registering for a business number, go to **www.ccra-adrc.gc.ca/eservices/tipson line/bis/bn-e.html**. For registering on-line, go to **www.businessregistration-inscriptionentreprise.gc.ca**. You can also contact your local tax services office for information about getting a business number and registering for the GST/HST.

Technology-Based Businesses

National Research Council

www.nrc.ca

(613) 993-9101

NRC oversees a program that helps small- and medium-sized businesses create and adopt innovative technologies by offering technical assistance and cost-shared financing of such projects. Part of their mission, in their words, is to take "a more aggressive, entrepreneurial approach to ensure the transfer of knowledge and technological achievements to Canadian-based firms."

Viatech National

www.viatech.org

Knowledge-based businesses can go here for free counselling in banking, legal, accounting, and marketing matters. Sponsored by the Royal Bank.

Women in Business

Businesswomen in Trade

www.infoexport.gc.ca/dfait

The Department of Foreign Affairs and International Trade (DFAIT) Businesswomen in Trade Web site provides a unique focal point on the Internet for Canadian businesswomen. The site was created to support businesswomen with information relevant to exporting and export activities. It provides a wealth of information on how to prepare for and succeed in the export marketplace, including direct links to other useful Internet resources and sources of information of interest to Canadian businesswomen.

Canadian Women's Business Network

www.cdnbizwomen.com

An on-line network that provides businesswomen with up-to-date on-line content, networking opportunities, and marketing options.

Centre for Women in Business
www.msvu.ca/cwb
Mount Saint Vincent University
166 Bedford Highway
Halifax, Nova Scotia
B3M 2J6
(902) 457-6449
Fax (902) 457-6455
Students attending Mount Saint Vincent University work with women clients on specific business projects. The centre also runs training programs and advisory sessions.

Women Business Owners of Canada
www.wboc.ca
A national organization that promotes sharing of information and advice and serves as a consolidated voice of influence on behalf of women business owners in Canada.

Women Entrepreneurs of Canada
www.wec.ca
A resource, support, and opportunity network for established women entrepreneurs.

Young People

Canadian Youth Business Foundation
www.cybf.ca
123 Edward Street
Suite 1404
Toronto, Ontario
M5G 1E2
(416) 408-2923
Fax (416) 408-3234
With regional offices across Canada, this non-profit, private-sector foundation offers mentoring, business support, and programs that lend up to $15,000 to eligible young Canadians.

Young Entrepreneurs Association
www.yea.ca
1-888-639-3222, (416) 588-0908
e-mail: yea@yea.ca
Seminars, workshops, and a newsletter are some of the supports the association offers members.

Bibliography

BizMove.com. **www.bizmove.com**

Carroll, Jim, and Rick Broadhead. *Selling Online: How to Become a Successful E-Commerce Merchant in Canada.* Toronto: Macmillan Canada, 1999.

Canada Business Service Centres, **www.cbsc.org**

Certified General Accountants Association of Canada **www.cga-canada.org**

CCH Business Owner's Toolkit Guidebook **www.toolkit.cch.com.text**

Gray, Douglas, and Diana Gray. *The Complete Canadian Small Business Guide, Third Edition.* Toronto: McGraw-Hill Ryerson, 2000.

Human Resources Development Canada **www.hrdc-drhc.gc.ca**

Investors Group. *Small Business: Financial Planning for the Owner of the Business.* Toronto: Stoddart, 1998.

Kuhlmann, Arkadi. *The AvCan File: First Steps in Understanding Financial Statements.* Montreal: The Institute of Canadian Bankers, 1981.

Index